IS THIS A DA

Molly and Tony were happily married, with a very nice home and two lovely children. Suddenly things went wrong. Tony spent less time at home and seemed to get irritable, even with the children. The atmosphere became really bad and Molly discovered that he was having an affair.

Tony moved out and the family fell apart. Molly moved back to her home town, where she and the children could be near both sets of grandparents and other members of the family. Once a month the children would go to their father's parents' house and he would take them out.

One day, when they returned home, the little boy said to Molly, 'I wish you would meet our Daddy. He is a very nice man.'

For Michael

Is this a Daddy Sunday?

Healing the Scars of Divorce

Steve Ann Henshall

MONARCH
Crowborough

British Library Cataloguing in Publication Data
A catalogue record for this book is available
from the British Library.

ISBN: 1 85424 253 9

Produced by Bookprint Creative Services
P.O. Box 827, BN21 3YJ, England for
Monarch Publications
Broadway House, The Broadway,
Crowborough, East Sussex TN6 1HQ
Printed in Great Britain.

CONTENTS

FOREWORD

Marriage today is under attack. Statistics reveal the alarming rise in marital breakdown, divorce and co-habitation. But behind statistics are people – vulnerable people like you and me.

I have been interested in Steve's book ever since she started work on this subject. She knows from personal experience what it is like when a marriage collapses. She also knows how deep the wounds can go and how long they can take to heal. Her last book *Not Always Murder at the Vicarage*, gave an accurate picture of clergy family life because she writes about what she knows, from the inside.

Steve provides us with genuine stories, among them some from children, parents and grandparents, which she hopes will help families to recognise and identify with some of the needs and difficulties which present themselves. Older relatives often find it hard to accept the changes which have come about in the pattern of marriage today. This book will give them insight from others in the same situation and show ways in which they might be able to help vulnerable couples and their children. I am both a mother and a grandmother myself and share this concern. The needs of my family have always come first.

Here we will also find a challenge to Christians in the way we respond to the problems which face us over divorce among members of our congregations. It is so easy not to get involved, when we should really be offering our love and care. Members of the Mothers' Union, to which Steve belongs, had to face this alongside the Church, when the attitude to marriage was changed drastically in England by the 1971 Divorce Reform Act. The tug of war between the Church's loving concern that seeks to maintain a high standard of faithfulness in marriage but also the best for the family still goes on. Family life is crying out for help.

In this International Year of the Family, I am glad to commend this warm, compassionate book.

Eileen Carey
Lambeth Palace

PREFACE
By David Alton M.P.

Not everyone will marry or live in families but at some time in most people's lives it is the family which provides love, companionship and security. Where family life breaks down, the community should do all in its power to protect and care for the casualties. I am well aware from the bitter sequels to family breakdowns that the resentment and recriminations can have far-reaching and catastrophic effects on estranged partners and children alike.

Rarely does a week go by without constituents consulting me about maintenance payments which have not been honoured, access arrangements which have broken down, and legal battles which have sometimes continued for years.

In this International Year of the Family, Steve Henshall's book comes as a timely reminder of what the personal consequences are for many of the one in three of our families who now experience the breakdown of their marriages.

David Alton
Member of Parliament

ACKNOWLEDGEMENTS

I have longed to write this book for many years, as I recognise and share the pain which divorce causes to children who are affected by the breakdown of their parents' marriage. At last, it seems that this is being recognised.

The ripples spread out way beyond the children and the immediate family, resulting in great unhappiness for grand-parents and other relations. Those who teach, heal and pray with them are also touched and sometimes distressed by the sad effects which are often only too evident.

The stories which they share here are all true, although I have changed names and some minor circumstances to protect their identity. Each one describes a genuine experience. I am very grateful to all those who trusted me, by talking to me or by writing their own accounts in such detail, so that others might be helped to understand both the depths and the triumphs.

Many of them are survivors, including me.

Steve Ann Henshall. 1994.

CHAPTER ONE

THE END OF A FAIRYTALE MARRIAGE AND DIVORCE IN THE NINETIES

The day I heard that Prince Charles and Princess Diana were to separate, I felt terribly shocked and very, very sad. I had been out all day and came hurrying into the house, rushing across the kitchen to put the kettle on. I switched on the radio as I went past and was totally bowled over by the news.

The tabloid press had been carrying stories about the royal marriage for months but I was one of the people who had refused to believe any of it. Even when the book *Diana: Her True Story* came out, my husband Michael and I dismissed it as salacious rubbish. We could not understand how anybody could take it seriously, least of all the couple themselves or the rest of the royal family.

The way that photographers tore round the world after them and rudely invaded their privacy on every possible occasion completely turned us off. We supposed journalists' interpretations of Diana's expressions and Charles' apparent off-handed behaviour to be purely a figment of their own over-stimulated imaginations.

So all I could do after I first heard the news was to sit down and drink one cup of coffee after another. As the radio droned on I seemed to be listening to the end of a fairytale. A whole kaleidoscope of pictures tumbled through my head: their smiling faces when the engagement was announced, Charles proudly piloting his beautiful wife through adoring crowds, holiday snaps with their two little boys, all the memories which signalled a happy family life.

Eventually I pulled myself together and went shopping, telling myself as I drove along that it was time I grew up and accepted the world as it really was. The supermarket was quiet and rather dreary. Other late shoppers trundled their trolleys along the aisles and I wondered if they were feeling as depressed as I was. As I stood gloomily surveying the vegetables, I caught the eye of the woman beside me, a complete stranger. It seemed quite natural for me to ask "Have you heard the news?" There was no need to explain what I meant for she replied immediately, "Oh yes, it's awful isn't it? But I suppose we should have seen it coming. After all, look at the difference in their ages. I never thought it had much chance from the beginning."

She went on to tell me that she was divorced herself. The age-gap between her and her husband had been the same as that between Charles and Diana. "It was all right at first", she said "but as time went on it began to be more and more obvious. We had different interests, different friends, a different pace of life." She said they had genuinely tried hard to stay together, more for the sake of the children than anything else but as he approached sixty they finally gave up the struggle.

There was something very matter of fact about her account, although she said she was sad because her husband had died fairly soon after the divorce. "Men often find it more difficult than women in the end," she said. "Perhaps they can't talk to friends about how they feel. They may be lonely." I thought, even as I listened to her, how strange it was that somebody I did not know at all should be telling me all this so naturally, with no embarrassment, in the mundane setting of a large store. I am used to receiving such confidences from friends and others, but usually in some quiet, appropriate setting, in a sensitive manner. As it was, I felt very sorry and wished that there was something that I could say or do which would be helpful.

Christian Attitudes To Divorce

That depressing conversation on that particularly painful day taught me a huge lesson. I knew very well that divorce had become extremely common. I knew that one in every three marriages was breaking down. I knew that other people suffered, apart from the actual couples themselves: parents, grandparents, other relatives and friends, but above all the children. I have experienced this myself. But among the people I know well the subject is almost always treated with great care and tact, because so many of my friends are people who share my Christian faith and ideals. Of course, we care very deeply about families who break up and we are often involved in supporting them. But maybe we are sometimes *too* careful to respect people's privacy, *too* careful not to intrude. Should we perhaps ask who we are protecting? Could it actually be ourselves...myself?

If I am really honest, I know that in the past I protected myself and my family from some very painful truths, about which I will say more in the next chapter. My childhood was overshadowed by the unhappiness of my parents, which finally led to the breakdown of their marriage. The effects of this, not only on my brothers and me but on so many of our friends and relations, was really terrible at the time and even after nearly forty years still leaves scars. Well – meaning people who tried to help were either pushed rudely away or leaned upon too heavily. The apparent rejection of us by my father and the bitterness of my mother added to the pain and nagging guilt which we all bore grimly in our inner selves.

My own solution was to repress it, behave as though it had never happened and get on with my life, wearing a (usually) smiling mask. When I married Michael, five weeks before he was ordained, I felt more than ever that I must hide my background. In those days I thought that a vicar's wife should have a perfect family 'pedigree'. In the years since then I have met hundreds of clergy families and I know now how wrong I was!

However, in some Christian circles there still tends to be a critical attitude when family life fails. We really need to respond with pity and compassion. In the gospels Jesus seemed much more inclined to judge the people who appeared to be well behaved, who kept the law, who were maybe a bit smug, than those whose lives had got into a mess. He showed clear, stern justice when a woman who had been taken in adultery was brought to him, towards both her and her accusers. He had a long conversation with a Samaritan woman, sitting by a well. She was left in no doubt that He knew what kind of life she had led yet He treated her with the respect due to her as a person.

It is no good pretending that the traditional stable family still advertised on the cornflake packet is the norm. Twenty five years ago over 70% of us lived in families like that. Now only 20% have that experience. We should remind ourselves that the present law does not protect any of us. We can be divorced against our wills, for no obvious reason.

There is hardly a family in England today that has not been touched by divorce. I often think that the Divorce Reform Act of 1971 was like a large stone thrown into a pond from which the ripples have continued to move in ever – increasing circles, involving not only the couples themselves but also their children, parents, grandparents, friends and carers. Some sufferers do not receive any direct support at all. Many are perceived as not being in need of any support. It is mainly for them that I am writing this book, which includes stories told to me by various people who have experienced similar wounds. In an age when divorce is commonly accepted as 'normal', it is often assumed that it has little effect on individuals.

I hope that it may bring some comfort and insight to those who are experiencing hurt and help them to understand that they are not alone in the situation. I also hope that it may help other people to feel compassion and concern for problems that they would like to ignore but which will not go away.

I am not a sociologist or a psychiatrist. I am not trying to analyse the reasons why marriages fail. There are many books on this subject and most of them are mainly concerned with the man and woman at the centre of the breakdown. I am interested personally in the human stories of those caught up in the resulting ripples. These are the casualties of divorce who are easy to disregard because their suffering is often well-hidden. These people matter too. They may not feel able to express their feelings. More importantly, they may imagine that they should not bother other people with their troubles or that if they do so they may be viewed as problems themselves.

However frequent divorce may become, each person is still unique and their experience is equally unique: their pain, isolation and (in some cases) guilt cannot be completely shared or taken on by anybody else, however understanding friends of relations may be. I am convinced that there are still many secret wounds which go unseen, that there is much heartache and distress hidden behind smiling faces, all unrecognised. Perhaps this is because society finds it easier not to notice, and prefers not to get involved in other people's emotional problems.

I have already explained that my own experience was painful. I know how good I was at disguising the hurt inside me: the bright exterior, the apparently confident student, young wife, mother. Yet quite often I come across people who brush aside my thoughts about such things with remarks like "Oh, do you really think it has such a bad effect nowadays, when there's nothing unusual about it...no stigma attached?"

I believe that it is very important to help those who have not been affected directly by marriage breakdown themselves to realise the need for understanding. Sometimes this can even apply to people who have been personally involved, occasionally the actual couple themselves, or to other close relatives. At a time when almost everybody experiences divorce somewhere in their family circle, it seems to be vitally necessary to be aware of the needs of family members and others who may suffer from stressful effects.

A phrase I often hear is "The children seem to be taking it very well." This has always disturbed me. Maybe it is just an attempt by parents and friends to kid themselves that what the parents wanted for themselves has not harmed anybody else. I can think of hardly anything further from the truth. How do they know how the children are really taking it? I could tell them and so could countless other children who have experienced the heartache and regret brought about by the breakdown of their parents' marriage. You never take it well, however you may hide your feelings from the outside world – or from yourself, for a time. I can think of many children who have confided in me how they cried themselves to sleep, night after night. We cannot, we should not, brush aside the feelings, not only of the children but also of many others in this situation.

Identifying with the royal family

It would be far too simple to suggest that the break up of the second royal marriage in months was greeted by Christians with prayer and by the secular world with goggling sentimentality or uncaring cynicism. I did hear somebody saying "I suppose the fact that they're doing it makes it 'respectable' for the rest of us"! But surely I was not alone in my reaction to the news. Very few of us remained really unmoved by the tragedy of it all. The newspapers were full of articles analysing the background, the characters of husband and wife, the problems of marrying into the royal family, and whether Diana would or should ever become Queen.

Media interest still goes on, following their story, keeping alive the memories of that fabulous wedding, the glorious dress, the fairytale Princess with her radiant, shy smile in the midst of all the wonderful pageantry, watched by half the world. It is really a nation-wide reflection of what happens in any family when they learn that one of their own young couples is going to break up. They look back sadly to the dreams of the wedding day and wonder what went wrong. Everybody feels specially tender for Mum. She may manage to keep 'a stiff upper lip', as the Queen seems to have done, at any rate in public. Some mothers break down, feeling a failure, somehow responsible. Maybe most of all, families wonder how Gran will take it. When the royal couple broke up there was a tremendous wave of affection and sympathy for the Queen Mother.

In any family in these circumstances brothers and sisters are jolted and afraid to take a second look at their own lives. There was plenty of speculation about whether Prince Edward would ever want to get married! Children naturally feel particularly insecure. It would be very odd if the royal children were not affected by their parents living separate lives. One of the favourite topics in the newspapers continues to be the question of what will happen to Prince William and Prince Harry. How long will it be before they are assuring us that, in their case too, it seems that "The children are taking it very well"?

Friends of both partners are thrown into confusion and embarrassment whenever couples announce that their marriage has come to an end. Some take sides, blaming one or other of the partners. This certainly happened, not only in the case of Charles and Di but also that of Prince Andrew and Fergie. It happened to my parents too. The 'know-alls' boast that they saw the signs and have been expecting it. The truth is that nobody can understand the complex relationships in anybody else's marriage. Husbands and wives often have problems themselves in explaining why things went wrong.

I was interested to hear people identifying with the Queen. One divorced friend of mine told me that her mother, who has seven grown-up children, was going round telling her friends, "Well, I'm like the Queen now…we've got something in common at last…three children with broken marriages!" Others actually blamed the Queen. A psychiatrist wrote a letter to the *Guardian* criticising her 1992 Christmas broadcast. He suggested that her admiration for Sir Leonard Cheshire, a man who bore extreme pain without complaining, showed how little she understood what was wrong with her own family.

Why was there so much publicity in the first place? I keep asking myself why, in a country where divorce is no longer regarded as unusual, people have been so affected and depressed by the failure of the royal marriages. I do not really think it has much to do with the future of the monarchy; whether Prince Charles or young William will be our next King, although obviously that is important. After all, it only reflects what happens in many marriage breakdowns where similar problems involving rights of inheritance become prominent (although hardly of equal national interest).

I believe one reason is that in being made to recognise the failure of marriage 'at the top', we have been brought face to face with the uncomfortable fact that family life in our country is in a fairly disastrous state generally. We have been used to a public example of serene happiness. The royal family has been a symbol to us, a mirror in which we like to imagine a reflection of ourselves. Now we are left with a sense of shared failure.

It reminds me of the disenchantment many of us felt when we heard about the real relationships at the White House when John F. Kennedy was President of the United States. He lost a lot of his glitter when it came to light that he had been consistently unfaithful to his wife. We felt let down. We had been presented with the picture of a happy marriage; a handsome couple leading a modern version of King Arthur's court at Camelot. Perhaps we should have remembered that all was not actually well under the surface there either, since Queen Guinevere had a somewhat questionable relationship with Sir Lancelot!

We live in a world addicted to TV. In soap operas like *Coronation Street*, *Dallas* or *Neighbours* we see fast-moving parodies of real life but we know that it is not real life. Can we really pretend that everything can be explained: that the good are always rewarded, criminals always get nailed and that stories usually have a happy ending? Are we looking to the 'soaps' for a world which we think we have lost? Is that why we mind so much about the royal break-up? Has the royal family become our royal soap, so now we are left with a shattered dream, disillusioned because we find that, like us, they are only human after all.

I think there is another reason, to me the most important of all. Somewhere deep down in our consciousness, most of us understand that the royal wedding was not just a glamourous spectacle but a very serious occasion, when the couple exchanged solemn vows in the presence of God and the congregation. It was sanctified: a holy experience in which we all shared. We like to joke that marriages are made in heaven. Somehow we want to believe it!

Past and Present

A few years ago the British nation was briskly reminded about 'Victorian Values'. This idea seemed to be very appealing at first, especially to church people. It made us picture large contented families, sitting round the table with father at the head, trooping to church and generally behaving well. After all, it sums up the biblical picture of the prosperous man surrounded by his children, living a good life. However, we soon began to realise that this was a very false picture of life in the last century. Charles Dickens wrote much more about the terrible poverty of his time, in stories like *Oliver Twist and David Copperfield*, than about the comfortable 'well to do'... Victorian values were not so different from our own today in many ways, when you consider the great gulf between rich and poor and the hypocrisy which our age shares with theirs.

But there was one big difference for married couples. Unlike today, the word 'divorce' would hardly ever be heard because it was so unusual. (Plenty of Victorian families did not have married parents, so maybe society in those days was not bound together in 'solid wedlock', and not so different from ours, as we sometimes imagine.) Actually, in over two hundred years up to 1857 there were only 317 divorces in this country! Marriage was considered to be so sacred that you needed a Parliamentary Bill to end it. It was also extremely costly, and very few wives could have existed independently anyway. Even when it became a bit easier it was still thought of as scandalous. I can just remember, when I was very small in the 1930s, hearing my parents talking about the abdication of King Edward VIII and this strange word 'divorce', with bated breath.

The Victorians certainly knew about living in step-families but that was because so many women died in childbirth, so there was sometimes a whole series of step-mothers. Today, it is step-fathers who are the 'norm', because children usually stay with their mothers after a divorce. The real difference is that death is final but divorce does not remove the living presence of a child's real father, whether they spend time together or not. When a step-father moves into the family, there are probably more psychological problems looming in the background as a result.

Now, almost every day, we read in the papers about famous couples who have parted, husbands who have left home, wives who have deserted their children. These are just the tip of the ice-berg; the well-known or the occasional unusual case. I remember reading an article in the *Daily Mail* (Oct 1992) by Jenny Hall, daughter of theatrical director Sir Peter Hall and actress Leslie Caron, who left her husband for Warren Beatty. Jenny was five when they divorced. It was her mother's second marriage and her father's first. Now aged thirty four, having been through a divorce herself, Jenny wrote "I don't think either of my parents understood what they were unleashing on themselves or their children when they split up." Her mother re-married once and her father three times, so she had a series of step-mothers and a step-father. The title of the article was 'Why my parents' divorce forever haunts me.'

You only have to think of the families you know personally to realise how nearly everyone is affected in some way, either directly or through relatives. In the present climate, even the news that your best friend's husband has walked out after twenty years of marriage, leaving her with three teenage children, may not come as a terrible surprise. An old friend told me how devastated she was because her son's wife had left him a few months earlier, taking their small children with her. "I'll never see my little darlings again", she kept saying, with tears in her eyes. Her son and his wife had both worked hard to set up their home, pay the mortgage and bring up their family. Then she met somebody else and was now living with him, so the house was to be sold and everything was to be divided up between them. The most painful thing for my friend was that the wife had made it absolutely clear that she did not want the children to have any further contact with their grandma. I meet a lot of grandmothers like my friend. Other relatives, like aunts and uncles, find family relationships difficult and confusing in these circumstances too.

Nobody should really be surprised at the present state of marriage. I have been collecting newspaper articles for years. They go as far back as an article on the statistics of divorce in the *Guardian* in September, 1979, with the headline 'Plain facts about broken marriages'. Other titles since then include 'What most children want is to be normal, like everyone else'; 'Single parents damage pupils'; 'Why divorce is grounds for a health warning'; 'Recession pushes up the divorce toll'; 'Divorce: children stay scarred' (July 1993). On November 29th 1993, the *Independent* published the result of a National Opinion Poll beneath the heading 'Society takes a liberal turn in the 1990s'.

There are plenty of signs which show how this liberal attitude is affecting our children. Fathers wander through parks, sit uncomfortably eating hamburgers in MacDonalds on Sunday afternoons, trailing round with bored children. These are 'access' visits. There is no wonder that in many cases both fathers and children give up trying. I am a magistrate in Liverpool city. In the 'Family' courts, I see plenty of sad mothers, and surly, dejected fathers. Children have become pawns in a game which they do not understand. It is clear that many couples who think that divorce is in the interests of their children find out too late that it is not.

I am a member of The Mothers' Union, which has been a stalwart champion of marriage and family life since it was founded in 1876 by the wife of a clergyman in the Church of England. We got used to being told we were 'out of touch' after the big swing against traditional morality in the Sixties. We have adapted our rules, after some heart searching, because we cannot turn our backs on what is happening in society. We want to reach out with love to every kind of family. The replies to a questionnaire sent out to grandmothers showed how many of them were affected by breakdown in their families. But it also showed how down to earth, practical and tough some of them were too! In the past I often spoke at meetings about marriage, which we all regarded as a permanent relationship. Now I am much more likely to be speaking about the casualties of divorce because I am concerned to help women to understand and cope with the situations they meet constantly in their family life today.

Some of the saddest people we are likely to come across are the mothers whose children only stay married for a very short time. They find it difficult to understand why they have not tried harder. They remember the times when things went wrong in their own marriages in the past but they had to 'grin and bear it'.

In middle age they can often look back and be glad that they did so because their relationships with their husbands have mellowed with time and they are now able to enjoy life together.

I suspect that Michael and I are not the only ones who half dread the family news in the annual letters we get from old friends at Christmas. It is often quite difficult to know how to reply, whether we should respond at all, when we read that they or their children are no longer together. Sometimes we can only guess at the heartbreak that lies behind the stark facts. Perhaps too many of us have grown up with the model of the 'stiff upper lip'.

The effects of easy divorce

In 1975 we spent a very happy summer working in a parish near San Francisco, in California. Our three children went with us. It was a fascinating experience in every way. There was only one blot on the landscape: the shock we had when we discovered that one in three marriages there ended in divorce. I remember coming back home and how amazed our friends and the congregation at our church were when we told them. We were all still comfortably secure in the knowledge that such a thing could never happen here. Well, it has now! We cannot be far behind the present U.S. rate which is approaching one in two.

Today my own country has the highest divorce rate in Europe with the exception of Denmark. Nearly two million children live with only one parent, usually their mothers. More than six million people live in step-families. These are facts which we ignore at our peril. It is no good looking back; there is no point in apportioning blame—the decline of religion, working wives, unemployment—these may all contribute to the overall situation. What matters is that we recognise what is really happening to family life in our country and accept our responsibility towards those who are wounded by it.

Society has made it far too easy both to get into marriage and to get out of it, without taking account of the harm this does to the individuals concerned. It is clear that most young people have very little, if any, preparation for what they are taking on in their future life together. I hate to hear the cynical remark that bridegrooms not only have to remember the ring nowadays but they also need to carry a solicitor's address in their back pocket. I believe that, in almost every instance, when a man and a woman make their vows to each other on their wedding day, they do sincerely want their marriage to work. If it does not, they and their families are devastated. Sadly, couples often find that the arrival of children is a shattering blow. It brings the question of sharing childcare and housework. This is when women tend to be pushed back into 'traditional' roles.

It is not really surprising that a huge number of conversations turn to the subject of the breakdown of family life. Sometimes these are with clergy, who speak about the difficulty of remaining sufficiently detached from the people and their problems to be useful to a family in distress. On another occasion a doctor will describe how a lot of the illness he deals with seems to be caused by marriage breakdown. Teachers are constantly aware of yet another child in their class whose Dad or Mum has left home. The teacher of a reception class told me that one day when she had seven new four year-olds she discovered that only one of them lived in a 'family' with two parents.

In February 1993, England was swept by a tide of horror when two ten year old boys murdered a toddler near Liverpool. It happened only five miles from where I live and he was abducted from a shopping centre in Bootle which I often use, so I know how it affected the local community. It was reported all over the world, not only at the time but again in lurid detail some months later when the boys were tried.

We learned that both boys came from broken homes and often played truant. There was other detailed and hostile information, including the fact that they were pupils at a church school. The country, the city, everybody, seemed to suffer from terrible pangs of guilt. Since that time, we all seem to have been thrown into a state of confusion, trying to work out what has gone wrong with our society. 'Family life' has become an overworked phrase. 'Back to Basics', introduced by the Prime Minister, John Major, as a slogan at the Conservative conference, was seized on with enthusiasm as the answer to all our troubles, as though we could just turn the clock back. It has been discredited, from the 'moral' point of view, as quickly as the return to Victorian values was before it.

The problem of absent fathers was further highlighted in England in 1993, when the Child Support Agency was set up to trace men who contribute very little or nothing towards the upkeep of their families. This has produced some dreadful scenes. Children of second marriages have been trailed through the streets in demonstrations with their parents, who find they are crippled by legal demands to pay more to the first family. Children of first marriages have seen their mothers fighting angrily for their rights, often after years of poverty, living on social security. Members of Parliament have been besieged by furious men and women, seeking 'justice'.

So the Agency, which was set up to help families, seems to have opened the flood-gates on the whole question of family life today in a way that nobody ever imagined.

Close on its heels came the Report *Children Living in Re-ordered Families*, published at the beginning of 1994, which made clear what many of us already knew: that the absence of a parent is much more harmful to the children than parents who stay together, even if they are not happy. At last society may be beginning to understand that individuals do matter and do suffer.

This state of moral panic is not peculiar to England. Americans and Australians, among others, are also in a state of 'navel gazing', as we look back on years of self-indulgence and the havoc which has resulted in people's private lives and emotions. There are many scars. There is much healing to be done.

It took me a long time to be able to talk about what had happened to me. It has only become clear to me in the last few years that I am now simply one among thousands. A whole generation is growing up without any knowledge of the extended family of the past. Older people often find it hard to understand what has really been happening. I feel there is a need to challenge some of the myths which have gathered around this painful subject, often due to people hiding very private hurts from those around them.

The experiences, thoughts and feelings which I relate in this book come directly from people who know something of these wounds, both those immediately affected, including myself, and those who minister to them. Some are people I know well. Others have started as complete strangers who have felt compelled to respond to my invitation, as I began to gather together material from outside my own experience. Quite a number have felt unable to tell their families that they were contributing. Some have talked to me face to face, while others have preferred the slightly less intimate medium of the telephone. There have been many letters, some of which must have cost the writers dear and were doubtless accompanied by tears.

They are not all tales of woe. Many show how the unhappy experiences of the past have been overcome and have led to determined efforts to work at their own marriages and the healing of relationships. Our stories are shared because we hope they may encourage and reassure other people with the same hurts. Others who read them may be moved to greater understanding and compassion in realising that many people around them may be carrying a hidden burden of suffering. Maybe by our understanding and care we can help them to realise that they are not alone. I shall begin with my own story.

How to deal with divorce in the nineties

1. Don't live in a fantasy world.
2. Learn more about how modern society has developed during the past thirty years, in order to understand present-day attitudes.
3. Remember that many people you meet will be affected by divorce, so take care to treat the subject with tact.
4. Be ready to listen and not be surprised, if somebody starts to tell you their story.
5. Take care not to be judgemental about marriage breakdown in your own or other people's families.
6. Recognise that some people may not be feeling as happy as they look.

CHAPTER TWO

MY OWN STORY

I had been up at Durham University for three weeks. It was a Sunday afternoon and I was attending my first college meeting. Just as I was recovering from my surprise at being elected as first year rep, I was called to the telephone. "Hello Poppet" said my mum's familiar voice, "I'm just ringing to tell you that we're going to get a divorce."

In that minute, my whole world turned upside down. I returned to the room where everybody looked quite normal, exactly as I had left them. The business went on: fairly trivial notices, reminders, particulars about the Christmas Ball, all the things which a fresher should find exciting. I even bought a second-hand blazer. But my mind was in turmoil. Everything round me seemed quite unreal, as a private nightmare continued to unfold in my imagination. A kind of panic set in, which appeared to go completely unnoticed by the people around me.

Divorce. The very word, denoting the final cutting off of all familiar family affections and customs, was frightening and threatening to me. Not only that, it was still relatively rare in 1952. The whole idea seemed totally unacceptable. I was hundreds of miles away from home. I felt completely cut off. I wanted to shout, stop them somehow. Yet even as I sat there, inwardly falling apart, the dreadful word echoed round and round in my head and somehow paralysed me. I remained pleasant, outwardly smiling. I told nobody.

Childhood memories and fears

I should not really have been surprised. All my life I had been used to my parents' incessant quarrels, often about very trivial things. My two brothers and I used to lie in bed listening to the distant rumble of their voices, accusing, irritable, angry and sometimes even terrifying. Once, I was so frightened by the violence with which they were arguing that I crept out into the garden and stood looking into the lighted room, just praying under my breath and beseeching them to stop. I got so scared that I threw a stone through the window – anything to shut them up! Then, of course, they both turned on me. They were both highly intelligent people, yet they often behaved like children, tearing each other apart.

My father was a barrister and was known as a very fine advocate. He had originally been a solicitor but later decided to study for the Bar. My mother first heard about his change of status when a mutual friend remarked "Well, you are going to be proud of Will in a wig and gown!" This illustrates the lack of communication which really existed between my parents. In later years, any mention of court was almost bound to cause trouble, with either scathing remarks or complete disinterest on my mother's part.

My mother was lively and attractive, and used to attention. I remember her twin sister, my aunt Marion, identical in appearance but with a gentler character. She died, six months after having a baby, in the same week that my second brother was born. It must have been terrible at the time, causing great emotional upheavals in the family. It must also have affected my parents' marriage.

My brothers and I were all sent away to school. I went when I was ten and they went at the tender age of seven. This meant that at least we were spared some of the disappointments and upsets which often affected us at home. We became used to public arguments. Once my father removed the whole family from a hotel when we were on holiday in Jersey, because he took a dislike to it – "Too full of young people". Of course, we loved it. Events such as half-term and Speech Day could be really happy or total disasters. I became naturally pessimistic, always expecting my parents to be the last to arrive, if they did, and never quite sure what sort of mood they would be in.

Family days out were approached with a mixture of excitement and dread. I remember one in particular; a visit to York. My mother took the three of us for a boating trip on the river while my father was at the Assizes. We went to collect him and watched the end of his case, proud of his eloquence but also mildly amused. However, mum was not amused at all but devastatingly critical. As we travelled home, the inevitable argument started up. We sat in the back of the car, not daring to speak in case we became involved or, as often happened, were somehow held responsible for the upset.

All I could think of was my very first long dress hanging up in my bedroom. I was looking forward to going with my parents as guests to a dinner that evening for members of the Magic Circle. When we got home I started to get ready. After about an hour I finally slunk downstairs and dared to ask when we would be leaving. My parents both turned round and looked at me in apparent astonishment. "Leaving?" said my mother. "Where on earth do you think we're going now? Go and get that dress off. We're not going anywhere."

Better moments

It would be easy, for the purposes of this book, only to outline the bleaker side of my family life. However, I should admit that there were also many good aspects, including financial security (although like everybody else, we were subject to plenty of restrictions during and after the war). We lived in a pleasant market town in a roomy, comfortable house full of books and antiques. We were all used to my father's briefcase and bowler hat and the legal terms which dominated his conversation. He easily demolished our adolescent attempts at political debate and most other subjects. Life could be really good when things were going well between my parents, and I remember some hilarious car journeys on dark nights with the whole family chanting almost all the poems of Edward Lear.

Friends and neighbours knew that my parents did not get on but they could not fathom or have much sympathy for my mother's unhappiness. Occasionally remarks were made by well-meaning people, such as "Why doesn't she go out and enjoy herself? She has a car sitting there... plays golf and bridge, has plenty of help... what a lucky woman! ...yet all she seems to do is smoke all day and talk about her husband." They were right, on the surface. But she had her own agenda, in the psychological jargon of today.

We had few relatives. Although my father's mother and two sisters lived near us, there was strain between the families. One aunt was a doctor, popular in the town, She married at the age of forty and asked me to be her chief bridesmaid, which I should have loved. However, my mother derided the whole idea of a middle-aged woman wearing a white dress as ridiculous. In the event, none of our family attended the wedding and a wedge was driven so deep that a relationship which might have been a source of comfort to us children in later years was virtually severed.

Mum's eldest sister Dorothy, and her husband, Jack, had no children of their own. They were very supportive of me while I was growing up and wrote to me regularly during and after my school days. It is rather sad, as I see it now, that they never had a very special relationship with either of my brothers. When I was a teenager I stayed with them often in Edinburgh and enjoyed visits to the opera, ballet and the theatre in the early years of the Festival. I have happy memories of the tram rides down Princes Street, late at night after a concert, singing some of the tunes together, since we all loved music.

'Uncle Jack' became a very important person in my life, particularly in later years, until he died in 1974, ten years after my aunt. Not only was he naturally fond of me but he also brought a straightforward, sensible attitude to my various problems. He was the one relation from the older generation of my family who was able to relate to my own children as they were growing up. I valued his support, his teasing and his attachment to us. I miss him more as I grow older myself.

Stability and security at school.

I have no doubt at all that I owe a great deal to my school, which was an Anglican convent at Whitby, in North Yorkshire. My family rarely went to church, although we were all baptised as babies and went to Sunday School. I never knew why that particular school was chosen but I shall always be grateful. At school I was given another model on which to build my life: a monastic ideal of shared talents and mutual support. In the eight years that I lived next to that community, I found stability and security in the very solidity of the rock-like stone buildings and the regularity of our ordinary, ordered days, beginning and ending in the school chapel. My favourite hymn for many years was 'Rock of ages, cleft for me.' I still remember the picture I had of that Rock, which was somehow also God, in which I curled up for comfort.

I was very eager to please and do well at school but at first found it hard to obey the very strict rules, such as keeping silence in the dormitory and between lessons. I was also almost 'over honest', so I confessed to every tiny peccadillo. Several girls in my form were vicars' daughters and most were from very stable homes in those days, so I was anxious to present my own family in a good light. I only knew two people at school whose parents were divorced. One lived with her mother and step-father and seemed to be quite happy. The other always looked very mournful. She told me her father had gone off with another woman when her mother was dying of cancer. It never occurred to me then that such a thing could happen to my own family, in spite of the unhappy atmosphere which so often pervaded our house.

As a teenager, I became more solemn. The sense of guilt which had been present in me over the years became even stronger. I felt somehow responsible for my parents' apparent lack of love. I think that in some way I tried to bargain with God, assiduously attending chapel, spending long periods on my knees in the school oratory before Communion, perhaps hoping to atone for my parents. Ridiculous as it seems now, I remember the scaring thought that maybe I was meant to become a nun (not unusual in a convent school, of course), confused by some notion that this would redeem my family. I should have made a rotten nun!

The gifts of stability and a disciplined, ordered life which I received from my school were certainly put to the test when I went home for the holidays. My parents sensed that I was happy at school and seemed to resent the fact that I now went to church regularly, so they turned on me with taunts such as "religious maniac"! One day my brothers caught me reading the *News of the World*, which my father always bought to see if any of his cases were reported. They danced round me chanting "Holy Jo! Holy Jo!" They also used to hide my alarm clock on Saturday nights so that I might not wake up for early Communion. It hardly amounted to persecution but no doubt they strengthened my developing faith! Both then and in later years the fact that I had become a practising Christian was seen by my family as a barrier. They chose to see me as a prig. It created a hostile attitude which I have always found difficult to cope with, even today.

Student years

So it was a fairly confused young woman who sat in that college meeting on a Sunday afternoon soon after the beginning of term. My Principal presumably saw me as the product of my highly respected convent school. My fellow students must have seen me as a capable leader or they would not have elected me. My Professor told me later that he had liked my lively mind but feared that I might get caught up in too many other activities and neglect my work. He was right. None of them had a clue about the agony that was going on inside.

My father was against my choice of Durham from the start, preferring London, where I had also been offered a place, as I could then be 'eating my dinners' as a member of an Inn of Court. I had originally intended to read law and join him but decided against this, mainly because I did not want to deal with divorce. I found it difficult to accept at that time, as I had been taught, and believed in my bones, that marriage was indissoluble. He dismissed this as squeamish, saying that he saw himself only as "an arm of the law". He would not give up. The only letters I received from him were on this subject. By this time he was officially living away from home but in spite of the divorce proceedings he constantly appeared there.

None of us could make head or tail of the situation. Mum kept in contact erratically, spending hours in the homes of a few sympathetic, long-suffering friends. I was enjoying my freedom after the rather restricted life of boarding school and tried hard to put the situation at home out of my mind, although it was always there, a familiar pain inside my skull. Most people had no idea how I felt as I was generally regarded as an extrovert with no obvious worries, who took life lightly. Looking back, I wonder how I would have fared in one of the modern universities, a decade later, when the rules which had governed society had been relaxed almost totally and there were few accepted structures to which students could turn. I am sure that the religious discipline learned at school supported me during this time. In spite of my full life and the lurking unhappiness I continued to say my prayers and made my communion regularly, in touch with both a nearby parish church and the chapel of one of the theological colleges. I was fortunate to find an understanding parish priest who told me, to my surprise, that being a student could be the unhappiest time of your life. It had not occurred to me that anybody else suffered like I did! It helped me to get things into perspective a bit. My other support was the acceptance of me by good friends, a few of whom are still in touch today.

Final reality—betrayal

The day I discovered that my father was actually in love with another woman was unbelievably painful. I was at home during the vacation, trying to catch up with academic work. My mother was in a psychiatric hospital, having driven herself there and refusing to leave until she was helped. I was already in bed when my father came into my room. He sat talking to me for a long time, almost right through the night. He said again and again that there was nobody else in his life, that my mother imagined it all, that he had never loved anybody else but her and that all he really wanted was for them both to live happily as a family at home with me and the boys. There was not much I could say. I was nineteen and not very experienced. Until then I had not thought there was any other reason for the proposed divorce except my parents' incompatibility.

Next day, he rang to ask me to have lunch with him at a hotel in the nearby city. When I arrived he left me for a while, saying he would not be long. I waited for quarter of an hour, rather weary, with no suspicion of what was about to happen. He returned, signalling to me to come outside. As I walked through the door I saw an attractive blond woman with a little girl beside her and I heard my father's voice saying, "Ann, I want you to meet Margaret." Even then I did not understand immediately what was happening.

As I write this I experience again, after nearly forty years, the pain, the indignation, the utter disbelief, the almost hysterical comedy of the situation. I did not walk out. I ate with them in a state of total confusion. I have no memory of what anybody said, least of all me, but I remember only too well how I became aware of the relationship between them. The child knew my father too, although I do not know what she called him. That was the only time I met face-to-face with the woman who was to become my father's second wife.

Breaking up our family home

The divorce proceedings dragged on for over two years, and led to the eventual breaking up of our family home. My brothers and I met up with my father occasionally, to go to the theatre or to have a meal. When we got back, mum used to examine us, always convinced that we must have talked about her. We never had, as that was the one subject we all carefully avoided. I still remember the three of us, sitting in a row on the settee, utterly miserable, the boys often in tears. They were in a much more difficult position than I was, because my father simply stopped providing any money for us so they had to leave their school. Eventually they both went into the RAF to do their National Service. Meanwhile I went to ask the local Director of

Education for a grant to see me through my finals. It was a humiliating experience, as he obviously knew my father and it was equally clear that he knew about the scandal which was sweeping through the town. I was embarrassed by his interest in me. As it turned out, he was kind enough to arrange for some financial help, for which I was perhaps not sufficiently grateful at the time.

Nobody really seemed to be able to help any of us: I expect they did not know how. Mum would sit for hours writing endless letters to her solicitor. I can see her now. Her obsession with my father made any other subject of conversation almost impossible. She made herself go through the mortifying experience of meeting Margaret, twelve years younger than she was, who apparently had met my father when he was the counsel in her divorce case. After months of frustrated inactivity, she decided to move most of the furniture out of the house to a flat in a town about fifty miles away. She then sold it little by little.

At the age of fifty, she had to fend for herself for the first time after many years of financial security. She tried, and often succeeded in, a variety of jobs but her unsettled mental state made her easily unhappy. She railed against me often, which only made me feel more guilty and inadequate. The only times I felt able to relax were when I was back in Durham, which gave me some kind of stability (even in the midst of exams!), although I always carried with me a pervasive unhappiness which I usually hoped to hide.

Adulthood and marriage

Neither of my parents showed any interest in either my work or my social life during this period, so they were not exactly bothered when I told them that I wanted to get married. My father wrote a brief, dismissive letter, obviously not impressed that my future husband, Michael, was going to be ordained. He arranged to meet us but then sent a message to cancel the appointment. I was paying a brief visit to Jean Rook's parents, friends of my family, at the time. The contrast between their active affection for and encouragement of their only daughter, (then a fledgling journalist, but who later became famous as the 'First Lady of Fleet Street') and my parents' behaviour towards me was strangely hurtful. When Michael came to collect me, 'Uncle Horace', a bluff practical Yorkshireman, walked him round the garden and told him in no uncertain terms not to let my parents ruin our marriage. I never saw my father again. He turned up at our flat soon after we were first married, when I was out. That was the only time Michael met him. He recognised him as an able and quite attractive person who had become soured by the circumstances of his life; possessed by his situation, somehow trapped in a tunnel.

My mother did not like Michael, either before or after we were married. She made it worse by telling everybody, so it was often repeated to me and did not make my relationship with her any easier. She seemed to resent the fact that I was happy. She also derided us for being Christians. Her animosity against my father, coupled with his attitude in virtually cutting himself off from us all, made it impossible to have them both at our wedding. I used to say ruefully that they would have fought in the aisle! Joking apart, I found it very sad that my mother was alone. We were married very quietly on an August morning, from Michael's home in the church where he had been baptised and confirmed. I had loved his mother, a deeply committed Christian woman, from the moment I had first met her. I felt accepted by my new family, with their ordered, peaceful approach to life, so different from the atmosphere in which I had grown up myself.

The next few years were busy. Michael was ordained and became a curate on the east coast and I taught in the girls' grammar school there. Both my brothers visited us from time to time, until they married. My mother also came to stay quite often at first but she invariably talked about my father, accused me of meeting him and generally upset me until I was usually near to tears by the time she left. It was difficult to steer a clear path through the emotional blackmail, intentional or not, to which she subjected us. I know that she told her friends we did not care, which was totally untrue.

We were living only about thirty miles away from my original home and I kept meeting people who knew my parents. It had not occurred to me that I would be recognised but I soon began to realise that there was now some sort of stigma attached to my family background. Naturally I hated this. Most of all, deep down in my heart, all I really wanted was to forget the whole awful nightmare and wake up one morning to find it had never happened, that my parents were still married to each other. It may seem strange and immature that even so late, by now a married woman myself, I should have felt so deeply but most decidedly I did.

We moved over the Pennines to a mill town, where our two sons were born. My mother found it quite dreadful and said so to shopkeepers or anybody else who would listen. She had to acknowledge that we were very happy and there were even times when she began to realise that perhaps we had something special after all. I learned a great deal about life in those years. Most of all, I had found out how important my own little family was and I was determined that they should not suffer as I had done. They should be enjoyed and given time. They should be loved for themselves and taught true, lasting values. That sounds very idealistic, of course, but we tried hard to put it into practice.

The family met again for my mother's funeral. She died of a cerebral haemorrhage when she was fifty nine. Such funerals are invariably fraught, emotional affairs and this was no exception. Michael asked if the family would like him to conduct it but was curtly refused. My father was not present but his mother was. So was his remaining sister, the doctor, now a widow. My younger brother was almost unable to speak for grief. Our other brother was angry, particularly with me. I was expecting my third baby. Michael and Uncle Jack, whose own wife was dying in Scotland, steered me away from the cemetery fairly smartly when it was all over, trying to spare me from any more unpleasantness. No doubt they were right. However, I felt that I had somehow failed my two brothers. I was the eldest and I was the girl of the family. The intervening years have not improved this situation very much: a sad reflection when I remember some of the fun we had and the confidences we shared as children.

Settling down—trying to ignore the past

My life for the next twelve years was largely immersed in our growing family and our parish. We had moved again, fairly near to Michael's parents. They and his sister were always kind and welcoming and we visited them at least once every week. This mattered to me more than any of us—there were even times when I was the one who had to insist that we went! I was so anxious that the children should know their relatives and a part of me relished the sense of 'belonging' which I found in their house. They never mentioned my parents' circumstances. I felt that my father-in-law must find it all most regrettable, since his generation regarded divorce as 'beyond the pale'. If he had still been alive today I could not have written this book.

Somewhere at the back of my mind I felt that as a vicar's wife I should come from a 'perfect' family with no skeletons in the cupboard! I know how ridiculous that was. I told very few people about my family background. Just how little all this showed was brought home to me when a teacher, a friend who knew me well during those years, heard me refer recently to my 'past'. She asked what I meant, and when I explained she said "I would never have believed that you had such a difficult childhood. You always seem to be such a happy person!" It took a long time before I could see that my own experience and hurt could be helpful in understanding other people. Then one day, a parishioner stumbled over our vicarage doorstep, having come to us straight from the divorce court and I found myself saying, "If it's any comfort to you, it happened to my family too. I do understand."

The horizons of the parish, with occasional short periods of supply teaching and the affirming experience of being used as a religious broadcaster were all I knew or needed during those years. I had no ambitions for Michael in a worldly sense and enjoyed living in the vicarage, belonging to the extended family which we found there. I knew from my past that money and position did not bring happiness and I was content.

Then suddenly all that changed. We left parish life for good when Michael became a bishop. Nobody else seemed surprised and most did not believe that I was. They did not understand that I was surprised, because I did not tell them that I felt so bereaved both beforehand and for some time afterwards. I had no fears about the public side of the new life, as I am naturally gregarious. In fact, my problem was the very opposite: the loneliness of feeling I did not belong anywhere in particular, as my husband's diocesan schedule seemed largely to exclude me at first.

Telling my children—facing up to the past

One day not long after we moved, I was sitting in the kitchen with my three children when one of them asked "Why do we never see your Dad?" They already knew that his second wife was not my mother but I realised that they assumed he had married again after she died. Strangely, this was in keeping with my own thoughts, since in a confused way I had regarded him as still married to her while she was alive. "Well", I remember saying with a great sense of relief, "perhaps it's time I told you the truth about my family." They sat there, my two sons of fifteen and thirteen and my little girl of eleven, listening gravely. When I had finished the whole sorry story, they were surprisingly accepting. "That explains a lot of things," said my eldest son in a matter-of-fact manner. We went on to discuss how it had affected the way they had been brought up themselves; the emphasis on family meals, family holidays, and above all valuing people more than things.

Another conversation about this time also made me think deeply. A friend whose brother had just been divorced began telling me confidently that the children seemed to be coping very well. He said he understood that such children grew up to be more independent than most, with plenty of self-confidence. I listened for a while, feeling more and more angry at this apparent complacency. Eventually, I told him that I simply did not believe it and described my own experience: the feeling of rejection, the confused, insecure anger which still surfaced occasionally, however bright my exterior.

There followed a year which I would rather not remember. It seemed as though all the repressed thoughts and fears of the past, with which I thought I had dealt so well, were coming back to face me again. Michael, who has been my strong support throughout our married life, was at first unaware of the trauma through which I was going. This was my own fault, as I did not want to upset his new work, which he was enjoying so much. He was not based at home in the same way that he had been as a parish priest. Quite often I did not see him for hours at a time, so for a while I kept my feelings to myself.

My father died of a stroke during that year. I could not face his funeral, aware that it would be thought rather odd if I turned up after all this time. Most of all, I could not bear to meet his wife and their son, my half-brother, who would be his accepted family. He had become a Roman Catholic towards the end of his life. One of my brothers telephoned me, angry that I would not be present. A week later, he rang again, saying "You were the sensible one. It was an awful experience." His death, while it plunged me into dreadful remorse, also brought a certain relief. I regret that our relationship was so strained in the past and non-existent during his last years, because I remember how much we once shared.

Some years later, speaking to a group of clergy about the Mothers' Union, trying hard to explain how the changes in its charter in 1974 actually meant accepting family life as it is now in reality, not as we might like it to be, I surprised myself. I heard my own voice explaining that we needed to reach out most of all to the children whose parents' marriages had broken down, admitting that it had happened to my own family. Nobody moved a muscle! On the way home, I felt a mixture of panic and pleased relief that at last I seemed to have laid the ghost. I had actually spoken about it in public! Ever since that day I have felt free to admit my past and realise that my own experience can be useful to other people.

Acknowledging the scars

There is just one warning note. I believe that however well we deal with our wounds, the scars remain forever, still liable to remind us of past hurts with a warning twinge. A few weeks before she died, we paid a brief visit to Jean Rook. It came about because we had met to take part in the same radio programme after a break of over thirty years, during which time our paths had diverged considerably. Her mother was there, by now an elderly lady. I was pleased to see her but soon discovered that her attitude towards me was very judgemental and hurtfully critical. She seemed to have no idea about the impact of my parents' divorce on me personally, and trawled up lurid details of family history, some of which I had never heard before, with withering remarks about both my mother and father. Jean tried to stop the cruel flow. I crawled (metaphorically) out of that house, mentally back in the guilt-ridden atmosphere of my adolescence. It took three days and the support of my very loving husband to shake myself free again.

I have been fortunate in so many ways in the help and care I have been given by Michael and our children, now grown up. We all have a sense of humour, thank goodness, so they do not take me too seriously, except when they realise that I am really in need. There are certain regrets about the past, particularly that I was not able to share more of these thoughts earlier. I also wish, now that I am older myself, that I had been more forgiving towards my parents while they were alive. My faith has under-girded everything, although it would be less than honest to say that I have always found it easy to pray. I should add that the help of a spiritual director with whom I could share everything has been invaluable throughout my adult life.

I have found it very hard to write about my own past and my family in this way. A few years ago I could never have envisaged doing such a thing. It has revived painful memories which I hardly knew I had. However, it has also been a therapeutic exercise, both healing and affirming. It has shown me that in spite of the despair and pessimism with which I once viewed family life I know that it is possible to heal the wounds, deal with the scars and enjoy a happy marriage.

How to face your own story

1. Write down your own story if possible.
2. Be prepared for memories and emotions to be stirred.
3. Decide if you wish to burn it, as a sign that it is over.
4. Don't try to repress the past because it often makes the situation worse.
5. Confide in somebody else, which will be helpful. You may need a trained counsellor.
6. Forgive and ask for forgiveness while you can.

CHAPTER THREE

SURVIVING SUFFERING: CHILDREN ARE OFTEN THE REAL VICTIMS

I used to wonder if there were other people like me, walking around with a big burden of guilt and pain which they were sure no one else could share. Now I know that there must be thousands because so many of them wrote to me! In fact, my greatest difficulty in writing this book has been in deciding what I should not include. I have been deeply moved by stories from people of many backgrounds and ages, by their honesty, sensitivity and often by their great bravery. We may never know how many of our friends and other people we meet keep their secrets closely locked up inside, hiding deep feelings of insecurity, fending off memories which may still come back in dreams.

Some of the writers describe very private experiences: women who feel they have suffered from damaged childhoods in the past, but have never felt they could talk about it. On the other hand there are others who have been shocked by the full glare of publicity or the interference of relations and friends. Somehow most of them have survived. They may give hope to other people who share these feelings.

At the end of the last chapter I suggested that the very act of writing down our feelings and experiences could be therapeutic, that is 'healing', in itself. One person who wrote to me explained that she was not used to talking to anybody else about what had happened to her. She went to tremendous trouble to write her account, in very full detail, filling over 22 pages. I think that even if nobody else had ever read it, the effort of remembering, trying to look at herself from the outside, weighing up the effect her past had on her as she grew up and now as she brings up her own children, must have been very helpful to her. As she wrote, she became more and more confident. I shall call her Ruth, because like Ruth in the Old Testament story, she faced the future practically and bravely after a tragic past.

Memories of a violent childhood

"If I was asked, I'd say I have survived and ended up happily," wrote Ruth after her long look back at a very unhappy childhood. She also felt "...it gave me the determination to make things better for my own children. An educational psychologist said in my son's report that he was confident, happy and emotionally secure. You can guess that pleased me even more than his super report! Indeed, I think that both children are happy, normal children."

She is a person who, up to the present, says she would not consider having counselling, "...probably because I managed to blank off the worst memories in order to forget and get on with life." Like me, she never told anyone about it until fairly recently. Then a friend who had been through the same experience told her about her feelings and reactions. Ruth says "...this was the greatest help and comfort to me – very kind and brave, I thought. I didn't feel such a stupid failure, knowing that this confident, happy and successful (or so it appeared) woman had gone through similar times."

Ruth was fifteen when her mother finally divorced her father for cruelty. But as a young child she witnessed dreadful scenes: violent fights, with her mother being punched and having heavy things thrown at her, until she was bruised, bleeding or often unconscious on the floor. Ruth would stay home from school to look after her and was given her first cooking instructions from her mother's sick-bed. Police could not interfere in cases of domestic violence in those days, so although neighbours quite often called them in the middle of the night, because they could hear Ruth screaming down the road, they could do nothing. She remembers how her father would appear, looking immaculate, charming, "…a real Mr Nice Guy"!

Her mother was Spanish. She came to England in the late 1930s when she was very young, partly to escape an arranged marriage. Her father was so angry with her when she married a non-Catholic that he disowned her. She had nowhere to turn for help during the long years of her husband's dreadful cruelty. One awful day she attacked him with a heavy stick, after he had worked her up into a state of anger and revenge. After that, she was so terrified that she and her little girl fled from the house. In Ruth's words: "We did a bunk — then there was the problem of where to sleep that night, not easy for a distraught women with a child in tow. Eventually the people who kept a corner shop down the road took us in. We hardly knew them. We slept that night on two camp beds in the corner of their stock room. I can truly say that was the best night's sleep I had for years. I still remember to this day the feeling of relief and being away from the rows and violence."

The following years were difficult. Ruth's English grandparents would have nothing to do with them and her father did not support them. In any case they were too frightened that he might find them and attack them, because of his violent temper. Her mother worked very hard to pay the rent and keep them both. Ruth remembers "although we were not starving, we were often down to onions on toast. My clothes were darned and I had cardboard in my shoes." This period ended when her mother plucked up enough courage to get a divorce and married again. Her step-father was a kind, gentle man, with whom she was not unhappy. Life began to take on some feeling of normality at last.

Practical and emotional effects

Ruth paints a picture of herself as a withdrawn child, a 'bookworm' retreating into her own private world, without much confidence, afraid to bring friends home. As a teenager, she began to overeat and her school work deteriorated. She constantly felt responsible for her mother because she was alone in a foreign country. There was no-one to talk things over with. She was not aware of any problems about this at the time but she now sees that she never really freed herself from the memory and fear of violence. A kind teacher and her more settled life after her mother's remarriage helped her through her last years at school.

However, her feelings of low self-esteem and lack of confidence lasted a long time. She says "It is only over the last six years that I have overcome this (90%) and I like myself, faults and all. I realise that I am no worse and sometimes better than many other people who are only too ready to put one down. I can recognise what my gifts are and what I am not good at and I accept it." She adds, "I remember it being one of the happiest times when I found that I was perhaps an O.K. person!" She also discovered that she was affectionate and liked being with people. She had not seen any cuddles or hugs in her home life. She never received any from her father. Her mother was not demonstrative but she never doubted that she was loved by her.

She had very little contact with the opposite sex while she was growing up. This meant that when she considered marriage she looked for somebody kind from a 'happy' family. "Worst of all", she says, "because I think I had never experienced it, I did not realise the most important thing of all…someone you feel such trust in that you can tell them all your thoughts and feelings – the loveliest, the silliest, the worst—and share absolutely every-thing with them, in the sure knowledge that they will still love you and never throw anything back at you *and* that they are able to be the same with you. You also need a similar emotional reaction to things without having to say a word…and a sense of humour. I realise now that I did not know what it was to be in love and perhaps I was just looking for someone I thought safe and secure."

Ruth is surprised that people often expect children from broken homes to be divorced themselves, perhaps because they do not take marriage seriously. She thinks that children of divorced par-ents know only too well the effects of marital breakdown and desperately want to avoid following the same course. She won-ders, from her own experience perhaps, if they may accept their partners' ideas on bringing up children and family life too read-ily and without question because they fear their own childhood was inadequate. She thinks "…it matters so very much more to us that we should make a success of our marriage and make a happy and secure home for our children, so they can have the confidence to make their own happy homes, where one can feel the love touching everyone who meets them."

Positive effects

Ruth says that since the night she and her mother fled from home, she has known that money and nice surroundings are not important. It was a good lesson for life: people and atmosphere make the home happy. She never takes things for granted. Her mother's success in working with no experience gave her the confidence to know that she could tackle anything too, if it was really necessary. (She is actually qualified herself.) Although she feels that she missed childhood she also gained from growing up very early. She has learned that help and friendship can come from all types and nationalities—all people and backgrounds. She sounds more cynical when she says that she is especially wary of Mr and Mrs 'Nice Guys' and quietly observes their partners.

Her own words sum up best how she feels now:

"I have a belief—no, I'd say a faith—in God, that He never lets anyone suffer any more than they can take and *always* comes to help in someone, or through some person, in the end. Therefore, though I have been down in the depths, I have never really felt suicidal as I always knew God was there and looking after me and it would serve a purpose in some way and would be alright in the end."

Other victims

Ruth was an only child, adrift with her mother in the difficult years after the Second World War. She had obviously triumphed over her sad childhood to a great extent. She has made a great effort to learn from her own experience and is making a go of her life, bringing up her family with a sense of security. There must be many other women like her, quietly getting on with their lives: private people, secretly moving on from the trauma of their past life.

Some have not survived so well. Other people's accounts of their parents' marriage breakdown from that period speak of the agony of being taken into care with families divided up, or living with relations. Girls in particular mention the big responsibility of younger brothers and sisters. One speaks of "bewildering teenage years", of trying to be helpful so she pretended to understand more than she really did, knowing only that "...divorce was considered a betrayal and a disgrace." She still feels insecure when she remembers all the pain of growing up surrounded by rows and conflict, which she feels had a lasting effect on her and on her brothers and sister. In her case, the misery and rejection of the past stayed with her until many years later it was the "devastating experience" of seeing her son's marriage fall apart which finally led to her own very painful nervous breakdown. She adds "But we are all broken at some time and the Dark Night passes. I am through it now but the effects are not yet over. I do so agree that there is suffering behind many masks!"

I received a good number of letters from younger women, now in their teens or twenties. Their experiences have usually been much more public from the outset—some were still coming to terms with their own problems. Today there are many others in similar situations but it is clear that for each person the pain is unique to them, very real and often unbearable. So I cannot say that Christine, whose story follows next, is "typical" of the present generation of children whose parents divorce. But I include her as an example with whom many others will sympathise and in whom some will see reflections of themselves. Her public pain is in sharp contrast to the private agony experienced by Ruth a generation earlier.

Christine—A family torn apart

"If only I had been there, maybe I could have stopped them: maybe the argument wouldn't have ended up with Dad leaving." This was what Christine kept thinking when her sister phoned her with the awful news. She was away from home at a conference. She spent the evening in tears, totally devastated, surrounded by strangers who tried to comfort her. When she got home her Dad picked her up from the station and she knew that their relationship changed; that things would never be better.

She was seventeen. The family had moved six months earlier to a council estate, after running a village pub where they had been at the centre of local life. They invested their money in a business which failed and suddenly everything fell apart. Christine thinks now that the final rift between her parents was partly because they had been working together for seven years without any outside interests or personal space. Her Dad went to live with an elderly uncle, so her Mum started divorce proceedings, thinking it would scare him into coming home. It did exactly the opposite and he almost became suicidal.

The tensions grew and family relationships became very poor and strained, as they all argued and took sides. Christine shared a bedroom with her younger sister, who kept playing loud records while she was trying to study for her A levels. One night she "flipped" and smashed some of them up. Then the whole family turned on her, including her two older brothers, who not only shouted at her but also kicked her. Christine said "I just curled up in bed and wished I was dead." She started to behave recklessly towards herself; driving her father's car from a party in a drunken state, taking tablets, and once she tried to commit suicide.

Her eighteenth birthday passed without even a card from any of the family, except her Dad, who lent her his car for the day. He had now moved in with another woman. A week before her first A level exam she had a massive argument with her Mum, who told her that she was no longer her daughter. She described in detail how she now felt totally rejected. In deep despair she went to a local shop, bought ten black bin bags and packed up all her belongings. Her Mum phoned her Dad and told him to come and collect her as she no longer wanted anything to do with her. Needless to say, she failed her A levels.

Healing begins

She felt very alone. They had never been a very close family, and had few relatives. Help came through her old friends in the village where she had lived as a girl. This was International Youth Year (1985). She could not believe her luck when she was invited to join a group of ten other young people and spent a month in Israel. It gave her "...freedom, peace and space." While she was there she had a religious experience in Bethlehem, where she became strongly aware of the presence of God. Back in England a youth worker helped her find a placement in the Lake District where she met other Christians who helped her very much. They took her to Crossfire, a great evangelical gathering in Liverpool, which led to her wanting to forgive her brothers. She repented and accepted new life in Christ. She wrote to her Mum and brothers, apologising for her part in the family upsets; the healing in their relationships had begun.

Next, she went to a John Wimber conference. His charisma so moved her that "...I was somehow drawn forward (I would never have gone on my own accord – no matter how much I wanted to) and people prayed for me. I was told to take Jesus with me, in my mind, to the areas and confrontations that had hurt me so much, and say to the people that I forgave them, with Jesus holding my hand. I spent the next forty eight hours crying. All the pain and hurt I had locked up deep inside me, the stuff I was hiding behind a mask of joviality and happy-go-lucky attitudes was being released. I had been baptised in the Spirit one month after Crossfire and given the gift of tongues, simply by reading *Nine O'Clock in the Morning* by Dennis Bennett, and from this I found so much strength."

Christine says that her healing from the divorce is not complete. The scars are very much healed, although still visible. She is close to her family in a new way, some due to her growing up, some due to healing. She remembers how people said "Well, at least you're all grown up...It would have been terrible if you were all children." She says "What did they know? In my considered opinion the lack of a stable home when stepping out as an adult, the openness of parents 'not needing to hide it from the kids because they were adults' was painful enough and I couldn't imagine anything worse."

She says: "As an adult, I find that healing is still needed. I have an almost neurotic reaction to arguments: I can't cope with falling out with someone. I can't accept the fact that sometimes friends just drift apart. Who knows what else lies inside that has caused damage to me as a result of that year of turmoil? People say I have very little self-esteem, although I am very confident in many respects. I suppose to an extent I can't believe that people really do love me. Although I can be close to people there's still something dreadfully wrong, as though I expect much more than they can actually give. Perhaps I expect them to make up for the years I lost. I feel I was flung into the adult world before I was ready. But then I find that God is healing me bit by bit, giving me only the bits I can cope with one at a time."

Unfair expectations of maturity

Christine's story sounds very dramatic but it shows the kind of family tensions that are around everywhere today, especially where there are teenage children. There is already a lot of stress at that stage of people's lives. However much young people may say they no longer need home, (and many do say that), when home becomes unstable and when parents are no longer there to be taken for granted, there is a yawning gap.

Present-day society also expects young people to be able to deal with really difficult relationships. One who wrote to me described her own experiences as a teenager, trying to cope after her father left home the day after his fortieth birthday to live with his secretary. Her mother "...stopped eating, thinking or driving well...she lost a husband, house, friends, mother-in-law...she had no confidant, no counselling, so I had somehow to fill this gap. We shared a bedroom with bunk beds, which gave her comfort but gave me sleepless nights as she would scream in her sleep."

She was also expected to meet her father's girlfriend and act as go-between for her parents. She felt that her main problem was "juggling" them, being used by them for their own ends. Her mother resented the way her father began to lavish clothes and gifts on her when she visited him. He took no interest in what she was doing at school and was so insensitive that he rang up the school during her O levels to say that his girl friend was pregnant and they were getting married the following week. Like Ruth years before her and Christine, a girl of her own generation, she was left suffering from low self-esteem. She wrote, "Looking back, I was a very bitter, twisted and selfish teenager." Also like Ruth and Christine, her school work suffered badly. She felt that nobody really cared about her and compensated, as Ruth did, by overeating, until she ended up "very fat and fraught."

However some years later she has been able to say: "My life was changed completely as a result of my parents' divorce eight years ago, but strengthened. I am totally self-sufficient in a way those who have had an easy life tend not to be. I am very happy and content and my ambitions are perhaps more realistic than they might otherwise have been." She has also learned to forgive as a result of her Christian faith, saying "I think believing in God gives one an advantage when it comes to forgiveness."

Teenagers who are part of 'multiple families' (see *Children Living in Reordered Families*) seem to have a very rough time in most cases. It is not surprising that they suffer more than most from health problems, difficulties at school and in their social lives. It is often hard for them to accept a step-parent in the first place but a third marriage, possibly with more step-brothers and sisters and yet another new home, is a very daunting experience. Children in these circumstances deserve our sympathy and support most of all.

Looking at Ruth and Christine

The different experiences and attitudes we have seen in Ruth and Christine are not only because they were a generation apart, pointing up the huge change from the way divorce was regarded in the fifties to the easy, accepting attitudes of today. They must also be seen in the light of their very different backgrounds and personalities.

Ruth would probably have found it difficult to share the details of her violent childhood whenever it had happened. She was an only child who grew up without close friends. Her nature seems still to have its very private side. She was able to think out carefully in advance the kind of man she should marry, wanting to succeed where her parents had failed. Christine's experience as a member of a very outspoken, rather turbulent family, was completely different. Her nature is clearly more emotional and dramatic. So it seems natural that Ruth still seeks no help and never talks about her problems, while Christine has been able to accept help and continues to need the support of other people, sharing her story with them. Both have achieved apparent success in their lives and outward self-confidence but are aware that it hides inner anxieties. They know that they are still very vulnerable just beneath the skin. Their stories should remind us that each person will react to their own particular situation in their own particular way.

Common features of children's stories.

First of all, I noticed that nobody said they thought their parents did the right thing in getting a divorce. Everybody stressed how damaging it had been to them personally and to the rest of their families and friends, both at the time and in the years since then. Almost all the people who have spoken or written to me have mentioned certain things which seem to be common experiences. The words 'low self-esteem' crop up again and again, coupled with feelings of guilt, sometimes with memories of real despair. Rejection is another feeling that often will not go away, so that people still expect to be put down by others, or doubt whether they can ever truly be loved by somebody else. This makes some of them unsure about relationships. I have already mentioned the physical problem of compulsive eating for comfort. This can recur when problems arise in later years.

There seem to be two things which emerge strongly from most of their experiences, although not all. The first is a much greater awareness of spiritual depth and their need for growth in faith. This comes out strongly where people were already Christians before tragedy struck their family life. In the case of Christine, we have a wonderful example of somebody helped by other people who cared enough to bring her to faith and to continue nurturing her afterwards. The second positive thing is the evident determination with which so many have tackled their own futures, strengthened by learning from the past and seeing a lesson in it for their own lives.

A lady in her seventies told me her story showing how divorce has affected her practically and emotionally through all the different stages of her life, as a child, a mother and now as a grandmother. She wrote "I am not seeking to lay blame anywhere...trying to see my young parents from my old age." I personally find great comfort and hope in her closing testimony.

"One of the lovely things about being old is that you can look at yourself as you were, and at others who loved or hurt you in the past, without being overwhelmed with remembrances. All our experiences have contributed to our becoming what we now are and I feel that they are given us to equip us for what God wants us to do."

How to handle the suffering of your parents' divorce

1. Deal with any sense of low self-esteem, or poor opinion of yourself. Face it by trying to deal with your guilt. Write down your good qualities and see them in a positive light. Learn to love yourself!

2. Remember that other people may be feeling rejected so take care especially if you have experienced rejection from family or friends not to hurt them further. Remember too that you are never rejected by God.

3. Try to accept and understand the experiences that have affected your life in the past or are affecting them now. Make a decision to get them into proportion. Live one day at a time, if necessary. Use them to strengthen your resolve for a balanced life in the future.

4. Be prepared to accept help, especially from other Christians. Work at deepening your faith.

5. The scars may not go away entirely, so be prepared for painful reminders sometimes in the future. If you have accepted that you cannot change the past but learn from it, you will eventually find peace.

CHAPTER FOUR

PARENTS AND CHILDREN OF TODAY

It often seems that when couples are going through the trauma of divorce, they are sometimes so taken up with their own emotions that they can easily ignore the needs and feelings of their children. I felt very deeply about my own parents. I believe this is what leads to the phrase we often hear; "The children seem to be taking it very well," expressing the hope that this may be true. Yet I have heard so many "children", of all ages, still speaking about the rejection and hurt which they cannot quite forget for the rest of their lives.

Almost all the people who wrote to me were women. I had great difficulty in getting any men to speak to me directly. Some said they would find it impossible to express their feelings. Others said that, in any case, men do not feel things as acutely as women. I would really like to believe this is not true, as I know many men who are both sensitive and caring people. But I have come to the conclusion that on the whole men and women *do* have different attitudes to many things, not least to the effect which divorce has on the rest of their families. It is very often the mother who has to shoulder the burden of bringing up the children and helping them through the difficult years. One story illustrates the problems that can occur.

The parent's point of view

Mary describes herself as "...a divorced single parent with three small children... a committed Christian and a Reader in my local church." She was interested in the subject of this book because of her own experience and she hoped that her thoughts might be helpful to other people. We exchanged letters, spoke on the phone and met face to face. She impressed me as a thoughtful, sensitive person who has suffered through the breakdown of her marriage and who cares deeply about the effect it has had on her children.

She feels that eleven year-old Simon went through a difficult time, lasting for several months, when he missed his father dreadfully. Although he sees him regularly every week this does not seem to be enough. She has to be careful not to exploit him because he is a pleasant, willing boy and he has taken on responsibilities for the family quite naturally. She described how he would help her to prepare for a day out by making a packed lunch and putting all the coats and wellingtons in the car. She feels guilty that he should be missing some of the carefree spirit of childhood.

Fiona is two years younger and had a very rough time at school during the actual marriage breakdown. She found it hard to concentrate and started to behave badly. She is now much better but there are still signs that she is disturbed. She blamed Mary for divorcing their father, even though it was explained to her that he had gone to live away from them and would not come back. There were other kinds of worries, including the fear that divorce would mean they would have a different surname. Mary says that Fiona tends to cling on to any fatherly man she meets, including their vicar, the father of a schoolfriend and their milkman! She feels this shows that Fiona longs for a proper father figure but cannot express what she feels. In spite of all this, she is the one who sometimes is not happy to visit her father for the day, perhaps because it takes her away from her friends. Baby Helen was just three months old when her daddy left. She is now three but has been very slow in reaching all her 'milestones'. Mary suspects this is partly because of the difficulties of their circumstances. The first year on her own, with three small children, was especially hard. She was "...still feeling very 'fragile' and often far too tired and very short of sleep. I often found myself being very harsh with the children out of exhaustion and depression."

Relying on other people

I was shocked by Mary's account of the way she tried to manage, with no money coming from her husband for some time after he left. She was given food by neighbours. The church paid her grocery bills. One day she was even offered money, not just once but twice.

Her parents were very supportive both at the time and in the years since then. But they had many problems of their own. Her mother had been desperately ill and her father had a heart attack. In addition, her sister lost a full-term baby, so Mary had tried to protect them from knowing that her marriage was in trouble and she managed this until after Helen was born. They came to the rescue and gave her lots of practical help. They live 60 miles away but her mother came once a week for three years and even offered to live with her and the children during the week, so that she could go on a training course. Her father has done various jobs around the house for her and has been a tower of strength in many ways.

They were very upset at the breakdown but admitted that they thought her husband had treated her "like a doormat", so they now seem to accept that what happened was for the best. They believe that the children are now happier and more relaxed. Mary agrees with this. Her husband came from what Mary describes as "a quarrelling family". His mother did not even contact her, although she was touched that a friend of his family did bother to offer some sympathy. Her two sisters, both Christians, were very shocked and upset at first, especially the one who was single and looked on Mary's husband as an older brother. Mary feels that her two brothers have to some extent provided a male role-model for the children, in addition to her father who has very definitely taken up the position of a father-figure.

Healing within the family.

The whole family has not only given time and care to Mary and the children but has also learned a lot in the process. Her unmarried brother really put himself out to give them time. He said to her, "I never realised how much strength and support we get from the family." They took the children on holidays, made it possible for Mary to take the two older ones to the Christian festival gathering of *Spring Harvest*, and also offered financial help. Aunts and uncles were also kind and sensitive, just offering affection and not asking personal questions. Through all the effort and love which everybody has given there has come about a sense of healing within the family.

Mary is now qualified as a teacher through her own determination and the help of her family and friends. She says "My wider family have all been wonderful, as have friends at church." She stresses the value of friendship, appreciating the neighbourly acts of kindness, such as mowing the lawn, fixing plugs or just looking after the cat. She feels very moved and privileged to have received so much generous support. As I write, hers is a story with a happy ending, but she knows that there are still plenty of hurdles ahead and her children must, and will, always come first.

Divorce in later life

The problem of literally being left holding the baby is usually confined to younger women (although it can fall to grandmothers too, as we shall see later in the book) but often the wife is left to help older children to cope. A woman in her fifties told me how her life was shattered suddenly one day when her husband and her best friend announced that they loved each other. (This is not an unusual event, as many people will know.) They went off together leaving her to tell the children, which included having to write to one who was away at sea. In spite of the cruelty with which her husband made the break, she has gone on loving him and has seen to it that their children have continued to visit him. They are all now married, so he and his second wife have been able to get to know their young families. In her case, as in Mary's, she has been upheld by her very strong faith, which has helped her to have a forgiving attitude.

One man who wrote to me explained that he had been married three times, twice to the same wife! Looking back on his life, he admits that he can see clearly now that other people have suffered as a result of what happened in his own life, particularly his children. His relationship with his eldest daughter seems to have been very slight except when she was a student, when he enjoyed taking her out with him at times as an 'adornment'.

The children of his second marriage were ten and eight when he left them and their mother. He wrote: "Because of the nature of my work, which kept me away from home many evenings of the week and a high proportion of weekends, my permanent departure was not noticed…" He also said that the boy, who was quiet and introspective, "…seemed to take my change of living without demur…his schooling and social life did not seem to be affected." The girl, described as a more boisterous child, "…went quiet and a bit withdrawn but did not cause any problems either at home or at school."

It seems to have taken him a long time to find out how it had really affected them for he discovered later that his daughter "…had certainly felt deprived by my going and her schoolwork and attitudes were adversely affected." Apparently she had worried a great deal and always wanted her daddy back again. Since remarrying his first wife the children of his second marriage have been to stay regularly and he paints a rosy picture of the happy relationships among them all. One is left wondering what the children actually think.

The attitudes shown in the last story illustrate what I have already said earlier about the way most men seem to view their children. It is well known that the majority of fathers, even when generous access to the children is arranged after a divorce, do not keep up their visits. Many do not support their children financially. In England, a new agency (The Child Support Agency) was set up in 1993 to put such matters right, searching for absent fathers and looking afresh at the amount agreed by those who already do contribute. There has been a great outcry from second families, objecting to higher rates which threaten their own living standards.

How children see it.

I went to see two families where young children have had to cope with the breakdown of their parents' marriage. They are from very different backgrounds and there will be many other children who will be able to identify with them. Some of the things they say may seem to be very harsh but they express exactly how they were feeling at the time. I begin with a family who live on a large estate near a city. Their mum has had to bring them up alone. Only the eldest can really remember what it is like to have two parents.

Living with mum: a jigsaw with one piece missing.

Neil is sixteen. When I met him he seemed desperately anxious to be taken seriously but he made a lot of jokey remarks. He told me that when he was asked to talk about his childhood memories at school, he described the death of the family budgie, telling it as a funny story. He thinks the teacher understood why; his actual memories were so bad that he "…couldn't bear to rake them up." He is the eldest of three and was six when his mother finally divorced his father.

He talked fairly dramatically about three memories which he will never forget. When he was still quite a little boy his dad was working on an oil-rig. He came home one night and behaved so violently to his wife, who was in the bathroom, that the children were terrified. Neil was always reminded of that because there was a permanent chip in the paint on the side of the bath. The following Christmas Day, his dad came in drunk. The family had been waiting for their Christmas dinner for two hours. There was a row and he went for his wife, knocking her about. Neil ran to a neighbour to get help. His mum left the house and came back with a woman friend who looked at his dad, by now sitting in front of the TV, got him by the collar and turfed him out. That was the end of their Christmas and their family life.

The third bad experience happened when Neil was ten. He told me that once his dad had left, he "…latched onto grandad." This was his mum's father, who was a real friend to his family of seven children and numerous grandchildren. He described him as somebody who "…tried to make everybody laugh and was a bit of a comedian." Neil depended on him a lot. When he died very suddenly of a heart attack they were all shocked and upset. Neil did not quite believe it until he went to the house, somehow still expecting him to be there. He took it very badly. When they all went away to Butlins Holiday Camp with his gran he realised that now their family life was going to be led only by women.

I asked him how he felt about his dad now. He said that the family seems to be "…a jigsaw with one piece missing." They had very little contact with him in the early years and none at all for a very long time now. Their mum was his second wife, as he had already deserted his first wife and two sons and is now on his third marriage. Neil commented wryly, "He can't hold a marriage down."

He would love to have driving lessons, money in his pocket – most of all a job. His friends at school seem to have the same problems, including shifting patterns at home. Neil said "Nobody's glad when they lose a parent." Some of his friends find themselves in very mixed up households, with step-parents moving in as "fathers" or "mothers" although they who are sometimes not much older than themselves.

His sister Karen is a quiet, self-contained girl, who explained that she had "…never been one for talking to people." She "…wouldn't know Dad." The only time when she really wishes he was still around is at open evenings at school, when most of her friends have two parents with them. She thinks the whole situation is "…very unfair and hard on Mum." She is fourteen and wants to be a dancer and her mum supports her in this. Her pretty face with its guarded expression clouded over a bit when she said that maybe she would rather not get married.

Sam is now twelve. He told me "I feel I need a dad. I don't even know what he looks like now. Boys like to talk to a male figure and have somebody to go to football with." The family meet up sometimes with the first wife and her two children. They manage to laugh at the situation, since they are all in the same boat. But Sam is a thoughtful boy, recognised as a talented actor already. He is angry with his dad, who now keeps a public house. He summed up: "He wants nothing to do with us. Marriage is a joke to him. He should care for Mum – she's looking after his kids."

All three children feel very protective towards their mum and angry that their dad has never given her any financial support. Karen reminded me that "…teenagers want expensive clothes." But they think that their cousins are having a worse time and have been able to help them because of their own experience. Their uncle has recently gone off with a woman friend, leaving his family stunned. His son went off to college in a state of shock and Sam said that his daughter, the same age as Karen, "…won't leave her mum's side." This family had always been very close, with plenty of time together, holidays and shared interests. Sam thinks they have had a greater shock than his own family because they were so used to having a father.

Both families are members of their local church. Sam described the congregation as "warm, welcoming people". He particularly misses the support of a curate who has moved. He had been a teacher before he was ordained and took a special interest in them all, supporting their activities such as plays at school and success in football.

I had mistakenly thought that Neil and his brother and sister might take it for granted that not having a father was "normal", since the estate they live on has a huge proportion of one-parent families. Clearly I was wrong. The other children I went to see are still working out what life is going to be like for them in the future without a dad.

Daddies only come home on Sundays.

Katie and Dee sat in their front room, wide-eyed and smiling, waiting to tell me about their daddy and how they felt. Dee was only three, so she soon got tired and lost interest after she had made her announcement "Daddies only come on Sundays". Katie was very different: an angry, articulate ten year old. She could hardly wait to explain how he had gone off with a girlfriend from the past. "I can't bear it. I wish the house would go on fire with both of them in it."

They and their mum looked back to the day they could never forget. It came as a terrible shock at the end of the summer, in a very special year. They had an exciting family outing in the spring, with a meal at a big hotel, to celebrate Dad's fortieth birthday. In July they went on their very first holiday abroad. Katie said it was wonderful. Then one day soon after they got home their world fell to pieces. They came back from shopping at Tesco's and saw their dad packing his case. He took them both on his knee and told them that "Daddy and Mummy haven't been getting on very well." He said he could not live with mummy any more. She would be very sad so they must look after her. They all cried. Dee told me "I was very, very sad but now I'm not going to cry any more."

Their mum said she just could not believe it. He told her that he had been thinking about it since the previous Christmas. So during all those lovely, happy times they had shared he had been living a lie. She said that after he left, she "…just sat there and sat there, thinking about it. I'd never thought it could happen. We shared everything…our home, our little girls…" He had gone to an old flame who he had met again after thirteen years and he told her that he realised he had married the wrong one.

Help from friends, neighbours and church.

Katie said her mum helped her most and she thought her gran helped her mum most. She added "She's brilliant, Nan." A friend who was a counsellor, divorced and remarried herself, was especially helpful because she knew all about the practical difficulties, and there were plenty of those! Neighbours were very good and their friends at church were understanding and supportive. They have a particularly "human" couple at the vicarage, who know a lot about family problems.

It was an ordeal going to church. Katie was glad she was in Sunday School because she would have been embarrassed to meet other people. Her mum cried once during the sermon because it was all about families. Mum felt lucky that people stayed with her and cared for her. They could not condone what her husband had done and how it affected her and the children. She realised that it would not have been acceptable at all a generation ago.

School was a different kind of hurdle. Katie had a friend whose dad left home when she was two. He came back but then went off again, so she hated him. Another friend changed her name to her mum's maiden name because she hated her dad too. Katie used this word "hate" very often. The Head and other teachers were very helpful. One of them told her that it had happened to his family when he was nine. All this was made even harder because everybody knew her dad. He had been Chairman of the Parents' Association and was very involved with the school right up to the day he left them.

Working out the anger.

Katie found the thought of her dad living with somebody else quite awful. She wrote a letter to his girlfriend telling her she hated her, that she hoped she would "drop dead". She sent it to her at work, writing on the envelope. "For the woman who stole my Dad from right under my nose." That letter came from her feeling of being powerless to do anything and showed her frustration and hurt. Her mum described the girlfriend as "…tall, attractive and fair" but Katie said she was "…fat, with spotty legs, a moustache and freckles all over her arms." She could only see her as a woman who went round "…pinching other people's dads."

As for her dad, she laughed when she said "He ran to his mother, big baby, he can't look after himself. Well, that's what

Mummy says …and I think. Now he's stopped bothering about us because he's living in his girlfriend's house and she earns loads of money."

Her description of going out with him on Sunday afternoons was a sad, dreary tale of trailing round museums, while Dee ran around madly, and she got "…thoroughly fed up with looking at dead birds." Her conversation was full of remarks like "…it doesn't bother me…well, a bit, not much" and "I'm not going to get married" and "I want to be free." But she also talked long-ingly of the past, ordinary things like how they used to have tea together and dad would be reading the paper. She said she might bribe him or blackmail him by saying she would not see him again unless he bought her a new bike.

Katie also said "His mum should have beaten him up. I'm very cross with him…could kill him…He's made a mess of us. My mum was working from home and we were getting to the stage where we were 'rich'. When dad left, her work went to pot. Everything… he's completely changed everything… it's different at teatime, different at weekends, we don't go out together as a family. He's left us in a total, utter mess, while he swans round in his posh company car. I wish they'd repossess his house. We're broke… mum's just got the old banger. It bothers you, mainly about the money…"

Her mum is a calm sensible woman, worried by Katie's fierce anger. She has not felt supported by her mother-in-law or other members of her husband's family, although they said they wanted to keep in touch. His sister phoned her once. She was even told "Grandmothers have rights, you know", which mysti-fied her since she would have welcomed more help from them.

Her husband stopped paying the mortgage when he left. The Department of Social Security chased him up but since then he has lost his job and refuses to try to get another one. He intends to do a course, so that he will not be liable to pay them any money. She has the choice "…to pay the bills or buy food, I can't do both." She says "Without my mum I'd have gone under." Her vicar and the local church have also continued to support her. When it comes to things like school uniform, she says to

Katie "I'll have to pass on that." Her attitude towards her husband has become more angry, much harder. She heard that he had gone to the Samaritans for help but her sympathy is drained, remembering his cruel streak and how he has treated them... She says it was "rotten on the kids."

Dee seems to be coping best of all...But who can really tell? Katie is a little less angry. She still says her dad has made a mess of everything and that seeing him is "...a waste of time" asking "Mum, do I have to go?" She has written "Big Baby" across his photo in her bedroom. They are not looking forward to Christmas, wondering whether they will still have a roof over their heads.

Other stories

I have been struck by the way so many children have named the exact times when disaster struck, like Neil's three bad memories and Katie's account of coming back from Tesco's. Another girl wrote to me "My father left our family three years and one month ago when I was twelve years old." A terrible picture emerged from an account by a teenager of the worst day in her life:

"After tea, two days after my Dad's birthday, my Mum told us Dad wanted us in the lounge to talk to us. We were surprised as this was unusual, especially as she wouldn't tell us why. The news was on...my father stared at the screen and would not look at us. At 6.30pm when the national news had finished, he walked across to the drawer and placed a box of tissues in the middle of the carpet saying 'You might need these.' We all innocently said 'Why?' The first thought to cross my mind was that my Gran had died. But his next three words were like a knife going through me. He said, with tears streaming down his cheeks 'I am leaving', slowly but surely.

"I can't remember exactly what I did but I screamed and shouted out that I was having a dream. I seriously thought I was having a nightmare. I wept and wept and wept. My brother curled up in a corner of the settee, refusing the arms of my Mum. My Dad was wailing in the midst of trying to explain. Our little brother ran out of the room and rushed to his bedroom with shrieks of desperation. He came back after a while. My Mum hugged him. Time stood still."

We all listened as Dad told us things that Mum had known for some time…he was going away to live with a young woman…it wasn't our fault…he loved us just the same…this was the hardest decision he'd ever make…he and Mum were still friends…the list was endless."

That mother and children have survived. She has remarried, after meeting her second husband through a group which she set up at their church to help and support single parents (CLASP). Their father has had a breakdown, so now the family are supporting him. However muddled and confused such a story may seem, it is not particularly unusual in the world of easy divorce in which families, tragically, find themselves today.

A *Panorama* programme (7 February 1994) illustrated the pain which children of all ages suffer when their parents' marriage fails. It showed clearly that many of them cannot express this in words, but it is evident in health problems and smaller things like bed-wetting and being easily upset. A sensitive, articulate six year old drew a picture of how he really wanted his family to be. It was a simple diagram of two grown-ups and two children. He spoke for all (or most) children in this situation when he said to his child psychiatrist – and to us – "I wish that mummy and daddy would be together again…I feel shut out…I feel I am to blame – if I wasn't born they wouldn't argue."

How to treat children involved in a divorce.

1. Encourage couples who have decided to separate or divorce to think carefully what is the best way to tell their children, together if possible.
2. Recognise that divorce may solve some problems but will produce others, especially in relationships with children.
3. Try to help them understand why this is happening and reassure them that you still love them.
4. Do not be misled by their outward appearance. Take care not to ignore them but respect their feelings.
5. Try to keep up friendships with other family members, particularly grandparents, aunts and uncles.
6. Encourage the children to keep on talking to you.
7. Keep in touch with church, school and any group to which they belong.

CHAPTER FIVE

GRANDPARENTS TO THE RESCUE

I may seem to have been hard on fathers in the last chapter. But my experience and the evidence of many people who wrote to me shows that in most cases it is fathers who leave families. Grandparents become more important than ever to the mums and children who are left to cope. We have already seen how Mary's parents came to her rescue, over several years, when she was in desperate need with her young family. Katie's mother said "Without my mum I'd have gone under." Parents of the partner who has left sometimes do not help at all, which can be very hurtful. Not all are willing, in any case, while others have no time to give or already need help themselves.

However, there are actually plenty of young families where it is mum who has left home, leaving dad to make the best of bringing up the children. In these cases the support of grandparents may be even more vital for helping the family to survive. They can give both practical and emotional support. Those who do help may soon find themselves taken for granted, just when they have reached an age when they are enjoying time together in retirement. If they are widowed this can be a lonely experience, sometimes physically tiring, especially if they take on a household where they are subjected to children's routines, with cooking, washing and broken nights.

This is often at a cost to themselves. I begin with an example which shows how great this cost can be.

Marion—mum and grandma at the same time.

"When my elder son was twenty, he came home with the news that his girl-friend was pregnant and could not understand why we were not overjoyed at his achievement! However, he couldn't wait to 'do the right thing' and get married, although we feared that was not the best reason for the marriage, and so it proved to be."

Marion was writing twelve years after all this happened. She said her son's wife then abandoned the little girl and went off to work away "…and so it was that my grand-daughter came to stay with me." The parents were eventually divorced when Sally was two and her father was granted custody of her. Marion was by then a widow of forty eight with a young son of eleven. "This meant that I had to become both a mum and a grandma, because there was no way he could look after her and go to work."

Sally is now twelve. She has known no other home and is a natural member of the household. Her father has his own house but often eats at Marion's and stays the night there too, so he sees Sally almost every day. Marion makes sure that he has the final say in whatever she does, such as school matters and visiting her other grandmother.

How it has affected life.

Marion writes, "I suppose it has made me feel some resentment – sacrificing some things I would like to be doing, in order to be here when she comes home from school. Other grandmas say how they love to see their grand-children, but how nice it is to see them go home…you can imagine my reaction! People say 'She will keep you young'…but they are not having to cope with adolescent tantrums and arthritis at the same time. I tell them it is more likely to wear me out."

On the whole people have been very sympathetic in their attitudes to her son's divorce and to her. She is a committed member of the Mothers' Union, caring for family life, and she has found great support and encouragement from most MU members. Their remarks, like "You have have been the stability she needed" and "She will always remember your home as a safe place" have helped her feel that what she is doing is worth while, as did "You have made a grand job of bringing her up."

"Sometimes it helps just to be reassured, doesn't it?" Marion writes. "In this day and age lots of grandparents are the main influence on children's lives anyway, with more wives working, so I think people tend to accept whatever situations arise as direct results of divorce. I do believe we all learn from life's experiences and are meant to use them in helping other people. I have found this to be particularly true in dealing with illness and bereavement and also with family problems."

The effect on other members of the family.

Sally sees her mum about three or four times a year. She has remarried and has three other children. Marion admits to having no personal feelings for her, so she had not found the divorce too painful. She thinks Sally has not found it painful either, as she has grown up accepting the situation, having never really known her mother as part of the family. But she realises that she does not like any criticism of her mother and there is obviously still a bond between them.

Marion's impression of her son is that he "...has never really been happy. I suppose as the years go by he becomes more set in his 'best of both worlds' experience. That is to say, he has very few responsibilities as far as his child is concerned, and is able to spend evenings with his friends (unless I have a previous engagement, when he has to do his own baby sitting.) He longs for a normal home life, I know, but not everyone wants to take on a ready-made daughter, and equally she would have to be able to accept a new mother figure."

She feels that her younger son, now in his early twenties, has been affected quite a lot by his brother's divorce, because he has had to share his home and his mum's affection with Sally. He sometimes resents her chatter and they both obviously enjoy the peace when she is out with her father, with freedom to do what they please without interruptions. They treasure this time, as she says "He and I have always had a very close relationship since his father died."

Summing it all up.

It is clear from the way Marion writes and the care she has given to all the members of her family that she is a deeply Christian person. She also has a sense of humour and is a realist. She does not get sorry for herself. Her story is one that many other grandmas know only too well… Her letter ends with a question. "Although I feel desperately sorry for grandparents who find their lives cut off from their grandchildren through divorce, I hope I have been able to put the other side of the coin by sharing my situation with you. If I had known ten years ago that I would still be in it, would I have taken it on? I suppose so, but how much longer I wonder…?"

How Sally feels.

I was interested to have a brief note from Sally herself, which speaks for some of the children who have not been brought up by their mums.

"When two people get divorced, they should think about how it affects the children, or they will think that it's all their fault. What is the point of getting married in the first place when in a few years people find that they don't love each other any more? It's just not worth bothering with.

"Then the children have to go through court to see who they are going to live with, or you have to choose between one or the other when you love them both. Then one of your parents gets married or finds somebody else. That really hurts you.

"I was two then but now I feel slightly different from my friends because they have two people to talk to when they're worried. But I don't live with my mum. I live with my grandma and I can't talk with my dad like most people can talk with their mums. But people who live with their mums don't have their dads like I do. Some of my friends have witnessed and suffered divorce too, so at least we have *one* thing in common."

A constant topic.

I sometimes feel that almost every conversation nowadays turns to this subject. One day when I called a friend I thought she sounded very low and in no time at all she was spilling out her misery. Her son's wife had left home to live with another man, saying she was "bored", leaving her little boys, aged six and nine. The youngest kept walking round and round saying, "My mummy left the day after my birthday." So it is gran who has to meet the boys from school and help her son with the everyday things, still hoping and praying that their mum's weekend visits may bring her back for good, which is what they all want. This friend spent years nursing her own mother and then her husband died, also after a long illness. She is terribly sad about the situation but she has good, supportive friends at her church and knows that lots of them have the same problems.

The older generation, who grew up with more stable patterns of family life, find it difficult to accept the ease with which parents leave home nowadays. They are affected personally as they watch the great unhappiness and heartache and the sense of failure of many young couples. They desperately want to support and help but know it would be wrong to interfere. They often suffer even more over the children who are bewildered and scared, feeling insecure, unable to understand why their mum and dad do not love each other any more. Sometimes it is hard to see them experiencing the trauma of moving house and changing schools and having to make new friends. Then they see the disturbing effect these things can have on the children, often showing itself in problems of behaviour. I was told about an eight year old whose parents were about to divorce. He heard that children from one-parent families often got involved in crime. Standing with his arms in the air, he exclaimed, "As if all this wasn't enough, now I'm going to be a criminal!" Hardest of all, some grandparents speak of deep heartache over the remarriage of their children and the way their grandchildren have to adapt to a new relationship.

A grandmother said "I am lucky because our son brings his

two children, aged seven and five, to lunch or tea most Sundays." But she misses being able to ring them up to ask about school and wishes they could still come to stay in the holidays with their cousins of the same age, who do not understand why their "pretty auntie" left them all. She feels angry, inside, that her son is living in a bed-sit while his wife has the house. Her feelings about her daughter-in-law are mixed. "She has not only rejected her husband but all of us, yet we have been such friends – or so I thought. She always said she could talk to me and respected me. I felt that I was closer to her than her own mother."

That account will perhaps ring bells in many people's minds; the memories of the happy past, the hopes for "what might have been", the hurts of accepting how things really are, yet the strong determination to see it through and be there when needed.

Distance makes it harder to bear.

Grandparents who live near their families are able to be more involved with them on a day-to-day basis and know the children well, so they will be a natural source of comfort when things go wrong. But since the last war and more especially during the last twenty years, people have tended to move away from their roots, often because of jobs, so the links become less strong. In a fairly small country like England, even 200 miles can seem a long way when you could just do with a shoulder to cry on, round the corner. In countries like the USA and Australia families can live 2000 miles away from each other so every visit becomes a special event. The phone is a great help in keeping people in touch. When troubles arise, it is often impossible to drop everything and go to support them, so it can be very frustrating and add to the feeling of helplessness and sadness.

However, the distance may be created artificially by a parent who refuses to let children see their grandparents. One of the saddest letters I received was from a grandma who wrote "I now accept that I probably will not see them again, so I have written a letter to them to read in the future, just remembering all the happy times – no recriminations and no criticism of their father.

I continue to pray for them and hope that some day they will realise what an unselfish person their mother is and how much she loves them both."

In this case her two grandsons lived with their father and her granddaughter with their mother, her daughter. The mother had not seen her sons for three years, despite a court order that said that they should spend every other weekend with her. On the other hand, her daughter visited father regularly. The father justified his hatred of his ex-wife, and of her parents, because she had been adopted. He wrote horrible letters to the grandparents, saying they had no 'blood line' to his children. He sent back presents, and returned their letters torn up. He also told his daughter that his ex-wife's parents were not her grandparents. The grandma still persisted by sending chatty notes on the boys' birthdays and by putting money aside for their futures.

Some months after the grandma's first letter I opened another from her. I could hardly believe my eyes when I read "I feel I have to share my good news with you and perhaps bring hope to other grandparents who have not seen their grandchildren." After all the agony her daughter had managed to make contact with the boys, who now "...realised that she was not the dreadful person their father had made her out to be." Now, their grandparents had seen one of them and hoped soon to see the other. The letter ends: "It seemed just like yesterday...we hugged each other as we used to do...My prayers and those of so many other people have been answered."

This experience should bring hope to other grandparents going through similar ordeals. A friend of mine, the widow of a vicar, tried hard to heal the problems which appeared early on in her son's marriage. Her fifteen year old grandson has been brought up almost entirely by his mother, who has encouraged him to dislike and be rude about almost everything which she holds dear. Her husband had adored him as a little baby. He christened him and taught him to walk. But years later, when she drove him past the church where his grandpa had been the rector, all the boy kept saying was "...that horrid place." He is very bitter against his father and loyal to his mother, resulting in a cold attitude to his grandma.

Margaret—you might never know how much it hurt.

A lot of people are walking about hiding unhappiness behind masks. Grandparents are particularly prone to do this. It may be through pride or simply because they cannot bear to talk about it. I mentioned my friend and the phone conversation, but there are many others like that, some with complete strangers. Once they have begun their story they find it is a tremendous relief to talk and are comforted to realise that other people have the same problems. I have often been told, since I have felt able to share my own background, "I never realised you had that sort of experience too. It's lovely to know that you understand what I'm talking about." We are wrong when we take people at "face value", without thinking what problems they may be carrying round with them.

I first met Margaret in 1986 at a conference on the Christian Ministry of Healing. I had recently injured my back and said it was difficult to sleep when I was in pain. She gave me what I saw as a little lecture about sharing the pain of Jesus on the Cross. I could not imagine that she had ever really suffered, but as we became friends, I found out how wrong I was. She is a jolly, intelligent, capable woman in late middle age. I was amazed when she told me that her eldest daughter, Vivienne, had seven children.

When she and her husband Alec told me about what they had been through I was impressed very much by their sincerity and the different ways in which they expressed their feelings. Each has their own memories of the pain they suffered ten years previously, when Vivienne walked out on her husband and their little family. Their story sums up many of the problems which grandparents have to face, so I shall include it in some detail since I believe it may help other people to understand some of their own difficulties.

Vivienne and her husband, Kit, were members of a very close-knit group in a charismatic church. They had befriended another couple, where the wife was disabled and her husband, Simon, had given up his job to look after her and their two children. When his wife died Vivienne dropped everything and went to live with him, leaving Kit to cope with their three small children, aged four, two and a half, and one.

Alec and Margaret were horrified. She went off to them straight away, travelling over two hundred miles. She described her anguish, when she found them "...just sitting on a settee with their arms round each other." Kit was a teacher, so for the next eight weeks, Margaret looked after them all, as Vivienne refused to return home. The children were terribly confused and unhappy. Margaret has dreadful memories of being told by the eldest, when she came back from shopping one day, "I just don't want you." Of course, she knew that all any of them wanted was their own mum.

Alec joined them. He remembers a long, long walk with Vivienne by the river, when he tried counselling her (a skill he already used in his work). They had several sessions, both separately and together with Kit, as he tried to bring about a reconciliation. It was an impossible situation. Alec and Margaret eventually took Kit and the children home with them for the summer holidays. When Kit had to go back to teach they paid for a child-minder, so that the children could live in their own home. Eventually, Kit and Vivienne were divorced and she married Simon, setting up a new household with their five children.

Guilt and anger.

At the time Margaret simply could not cope with Vivienne's rejection of the children. She asked herself constantly "What haven't I done that she could behave like this?" She saw her "...falling short of the ideals of motherhood" and felt full of distress and moral indignation. She could not bring herself to see Vivienne for a long time, although she does so regularly now, but she is still aware of the strength of anger present in her. She thinks that Vivienne knows this too. She sees her as highly selfish and manipulative.

Alec and Margaret both told me that they had been shocked by the way Kit "...didn't defend his end but just dissolved" and was very dependent on their support. He had an unhappy background with no idea of stability. When he was a child his mother was constantly unfaithful to his father, so now he just seemed to accept that his wife was doing the same thing. He did not feel fulfilled as a teacher. He and Vivienne were very different from each other emotionally: he did not know how to communicate his thoughts, but retreated into silence. He told Alec that before she had left she had been very hyped up, as though she was on drugs, singing all the time in a very high voice.

Alec sees this as a "...desperate scream, some kind of seeking for release." Vivienne had married Kit five years earlier and had a baby straight away with the other two following very quickly. She said that she felt exploited sexually by her husband. She worked as a nurse several nights a week to help to pay the mortgage. Alec believes that she "flipped". She became so divorced from reality that at one point she suggested that the right way forward should be for all three parents and the five children to live together in a community, affirming one another. Margaret described Vivienne and Simon at this time as a "very Sixties pair who looked then like 'Travellers' [homeless people] do today. They grew up in a very permissive age when sexual attitudes were different from ours."

She believes that the religious element made it much more difficult. The church to which the two couples had originally belonged split over the situation. They were driven out. Vivienne had tried quoting the Bible at them to justify the situation. When Alec got in touch with the leaders he found them very critical, even saying that Simon had not really cared enough for his first wife.

Vivienne's brother and sister were very angry about the whole affair, especially at the pain caused to their parents. There was a tremendous gathering of loyalty to their mother: "How could she do this to Mum?" At first they planned to send a joint family letter to Vivienne, saying they hoped she would go back to Kit and the children, but they did not pursue this idea.

Settled family life.

Ten years on, Margaret can look back on the past more calmly than she felt at the time. The picture of Simon and Vivienne now, with two more children of their own, is of "…a compatible couple, very stable and sound, loving parents bringing up a solid, middle-class family." They are responsible members of their local community, attend their parish church together as a family and are very involved with the youth work there, taking them off to the Greenbelt Christian festival in the summer. They also have a high profile in the life of the local school and are very ambitious for their children. Margaret finds it extraordinary that they are members of the third order of a religious community, when as far as she can see they "…don't even see anything to be forgiven about." Alec thinks they benefit from the support they receive from this connection.

Kit is now happily married to a former girlfriend and has no more children. He has his own children to stay each holiday and gives some financial assistance to Vivienne and Simon. Margaret thinks he is more than generous because he also welcomes Simon's children to his home "…sons of the man who took his wife."

When they consider their own attitudes to Vivienne's behaviour, Alec says he thinks Margaret is hard on her daughters, soft on her son, while he admits that he is the opposite. They find their assorted "grandchildren", among whom they include all seven, are more self-reliant than their own children ever were. They do not seem to be emotionally starved at home. They all fight for each other, protecting the family, each having had to find his or her own place. They certainly seem to need Alec and Margaret, to whom all look as their grandparents. Alec gets on wonderfully with the little ones. He says the child who appears to need affection most is not one of Vivienne's but Simon's second child, who still wants to be cuddled, perhaps because she missed out as a baby when her mother died.

Providing stability

The role of grandparents in this family is to be "uniting". They have a "…very positive policy of relating to the children" and say that they are their "first concern, through thick and thin." The divorce has left a web of complex relationships among the children. The two younger ones are half-brother and sister to all the others, but the other five have more complicated relationships. So it is not uncommon to hear a child saying "I'm the eldest of yours and Mummy's children, aren't I, but Peter only belongs to you, Daddy." There are lots of cross currents, as the children go to stay with various relations from different sides of the family. They are becoming more aware of mysterious, obscure people, aunts and uncles, cousins they have never met. These are shadows in the background, on the outer edge of their lives. Margaret said "Nobody asks how they feel, but you see them coming to their own mind about all this and they may not see it in the same way as their parents."

Their eldest grandchild, Simon's son, has recently decided that he ought to search out the family he has lost, including the eight cousins he has not seen since his mother died. He feels the need to belong and be valued. This also means finding his maternal grandmother. She had come when her daughter died to see if she could help Simon with the children. When she found that he had someone else's wife living with him she left in disgust and has never seen them again. Now the fear is that the lad may be rejected.

Margaret admits that she still feels upset and angry about the situation at times, but Alec feels less so. They look back on the actual period when they were experiencing so much pain and remember being in "...a whirl of emotion." Eventually they went for counselling themselves, as they found they could no longer communicate with each other. Some old and trusted friends helped them to find the right person, a psychotherapist, to whom they went several times. Margaret says that it was both painful and revealing. It helped at the time but she still admits to some residual feeling. As they continued with the counselling, it became clear that their own relationship was also beginning to be examined in depth. They can still find themselves with emotional blockages.

Facing it all over again.

Four years ago their son, Robert, rang up to say that he had come home to find a note from his wife saying "Packed everything and I'm leaving you." They had been married for less than three years. This time Alec said he had seen it coming. Their daughter-in-law was an actress, with a blossoming career. Robert wanted a home and family. Margaret said she felt guilty because she had "...watched them flying in opposite directions" and wondered if she should say anything but had not dared to offer advice.

This time, their support was needed in a rather different way and it was a much greater financial burden. Alec lent Robert a large amount of money so that he could at least keep his house, as he had to give his wife half of everything he had. Their main way of helping was in listening, letting him talk when he rang up, often weeping. They have been beside him as he has gradually come back to Christianity, exploring himself and trying to find a framework which makes sense of himself. Alec smiled as he described Robert as "unendingly analytical."

They agree that they could hardly have endured two more different divorces. They also say that they were equally painful. Most surprising of all, but perhaps it should not be, is the fact that the first person Robert went to after his wife left him was Vivienne. It was her family who comforted him, her children who cuddled him. It was Simon's youngest child who gave him his teddy bear.

Alec and Margaret may look like any other grandparents out for the day, if you meet them with Vivienne and Simon and their seven children. Perhaps in future we should look a little more carefully at such families, to see what else may lie behind the happy smiles.

How grandparents can help.

1. Always try to remember that it is not the children's fault.
2. Be prepared to experience guilt and anger but take care not to let them take over.
3. Give the right kind of help, whatever is actually wanted.
4. Avoid giving advice, unless asked.
5. Don't be afraid of talking to trusted friends or receiving counselling.
6. Don't let it destroy the relationships in your own home.
7. Be patient if relationships are bad. Time often changes this situation.

CHAPTER SIX

THE WIDER FAMILY: FACING THE ISSUES NOW AND IN THE FUTURE

"What I would love you to stress in your book is the ramifications of divorce on all the other people involved. All too often it's not only the husband and wife who are divorced – it's all the other relationships too. We all take these for granted, until they're under threat. Every family has their own story to tell. It's easier when there is a perceived 'bad guy' or 'bad girl' to blame, but this is not always the case. Then the extended family is left slightly uncertain as to their new role towards the ex-spouse."

That was how Nell started her letter to me. She has direct experience of what she calls "...the debris of divorce", as both her sisters have broken marriages. In each case the wider family has been and still is involved. She paints a graphic picture of their mixed emotions: endless unhappiness, problems and anguish engulf them all. "No-one knows the new rules of play...everyone is uncertain as to how to behave...it's this sort of mess that nobody quite expects until it's happening." She asks "What else goes out when the spouse goes?"

There are many families who share this experience, even if they are only on the very edge of all the turmoil. Couples who divorce are often so bound up in their own stormy affairs that they hardly even think how anybody else may be affected. I wish much more care could be given by counsellors or other advisors to talk through the issues with them at some length, as early as possible. They should be made to face those situations and relationships which will go on being upsetting for years in the future, not only for themselves but for other members of their families too.

Sisters and brothers of divorced people find it difficult to know how to relate to ex-husbands and wives. Their children are often confused when a favourite uncle or aunt disappears from their lives or if he or she comes to their family for help. One woman wrote that her ex brother-in-law "...still comes to the house, walks the dog, plays with the kids." Her husband "...has had enough of the family marriage hassles in our home and has banned visits from my emotionally uptight sister for some years now. It causes a split that is not of my choice, resented by my sister, but understood by my parents." The generation "in the middle" have the greatest dilemma of all. They still have to be sympathetic towards their parents but also loving and caring to the rest of the family, especially their own children and their nephews and nieces.

A divorce in the family will obviously affect a great number of relations who will react in a variety of ways. Some will be sad and try to help. Others, perhaps not sure what to do, will keep their distance and say nothing. Past relationships can also raise some fairly thorny questions, such as how to treat the parents of 'ex' in-laws, who may go to the same church or group, and whether to send Christmas cards to them. Family weddings and funerals are the most "dangerous" occasions, when such problems are most likely to surface. Even the question of where various people should sit in the church and who should be placed next to them can become a minefield.

The trauma of being supportive parents.

There is great stress on grandparents, but cases of marriage breakdown where there are no children also affects that generation very deeply. They often spend long hours trying to see if the marriage can be saved. They are also the ones who are likely to be called on for help, especially when a daughter is in trouble, with practical details like finding the right solicitor and how and where to live. A mother who had to shoulder such a burden for her daughter wrote "...we went back and forth to Lincolnshire, hiring a van to take furniture down and help her sort out the house and garden. It was a very emotional stressful time. I spoke to her on the phone every night."

Parents will probably have to deal with the sense of loss and failure which are almost bound to be around, both for the "bereaved" wife or husband and for themselves. Some may have been half expecting the breakdown but others are shattered. I had many letters with expressions like "We were extremely shocked to hear the news as we thought they were reasonably happy...they seemed so well suited." One mother wrote, "It breaks my heart to see her so ill. I encourage her with letters and helpful books and assure that life will get better...but I find it difficult sometimes to believe that myself." Another mother whose son had been deserted, told me how much she still loved her daughter-in-law. They met up to talk it over and threw their arms round each other and then both burst into tears. Eventually she had to accept that when women have careers it is easier to split from a husband. She and her husband were left to work hard, helping their son to emerge from his tearful depression.

Fathers seem to find it more difficult to cope. One woman told me how she arrived back from helping her desperately unhappy daughter, "...very confused, upset and frustrated" to find that her husband thought she should have done more to help her so they ended up having a dreadful row. She thought it was because he could not go to her himself and felt powerless and angry because their son-in-law would not talk to them or reply to their messages. He had been so happy about the wedding and the two men had got on really well together. A couple whose daughter often appeared bruised, with a black eye or damaged hand, described how they went through agonies, feeling sure she was being knocked about by her husband. She denied this for ages, staying loyal to him, but in the end she divorced him. Her father was terribly upset and blamed himself, saying that he should have refused to let her marry him. He adores all his daughters and this experience has made him much more fearful and protective towards them.

Pauline and Louise—Brief marriage and early divorce.

A few years ago, I was shocked when a photographer told me he always insisted on being paid in advance for wedding photographs. "Some couples never even bother to collect them nowadays", he said. "They get disillusioned very quickly."

Pauline is a very pleasant, outgoing woman, devoted to her home and family and to her parish church. She described the wedding of her eldest daughter, Louise, as a "gloriously happy day...a full top-hat affair with no expense spared!" Louise looked beautiful on the arm of her handsome father, Mike, followed by her three sisters. The church was full of friends because this is a well-loved family, at the heart of an affectionate congregation.

Pauline was sad that the wedding plans had not brought their family a bit closer to the family of Peter, Louise's bridegroom. His parents were divorced but even his mother did not seem really interested. They were not practising Christians, so she often felt that they were "...not speaking the same language." At the reception they behaved oddly, showing off and not mixing with the other guests. Peter actually spent very little time with Louise and Pauline was embarrassed and found herself making excuses, even to Louise herself. She understands, looking back, that her pretty daughter, new bride as she was, needed comfort even then but she did not realise it. Next day, at a barbecue at Peter's mother's house, Pauline overheard her saying "This is Peter's wife", adding softly, "She isn't good enough for him." In spite of what appeared to be a marvellous honeymoon with bubbly postcards from the couple, she sees now that the seeds of the unhappiness that followed were already apparent even as they were actually celebrating their marriage.

A few months after the wedding, Pauline had to face the fact that Louise was very unhappy. Peter was tied up in his work and hardly seemed to bother with her. She was doing a temporary job and he put her down with remarks like "Anyway, I'm the important one." One night he completely ignored her by taking somebody else to a social event for his firm. All this began to come out when Louise eventually broke down and started to tell her mum what she was going through. Pauline thought of that wonderful service such a short time ago, the marriage vows "for better for worse", as Louise asked tearfully "Is this what married life is like?"

They were both terribly upset. Pauline was desperate to help her but did not know how. Should they talk to Peter? Louise said "No". Should they talk to his father? "No, it would only make matters worse." She suspected mental cruelty and found it heartrending to see her trying so hard. Louise said she would do absolutely anything to put things right. Their family had always said that you could get over anything if only you just talked it over together, but Peter would not listen to her or discuss anything at all.

Pauline told me she would never forget the phone call: "Peter's left me." She said "I got in the car, drove straight there and brought her home...something I'd been longing to do." The situation could no longer be hidden. Louise begged them: "Keep things smooth. It might turn out." She went on hoping against hope. Peter's father visited him and came to tell them that it was like talking to a brick wall. They heard that his mother was actually pleased that the marriage appeared to be falling apart. Peter's best man tried to help, knowing that he was a difficult and complex person. But when he turned up with another girl, he knew that a reconciliation was impossible.

Effect on the family and friends

The whole family worked hard at being loving and supportive to Louise, who still loved Peter and told them "I'm waiting for him." Pauline made excuses for him, explaining that he must be desperately unhappy and disturbed. She and her husband, Mike, were anxious not to upset their own parents, who all doted on Louise. They realised they were in need themselves and asked their vicar for help and advice. He was a tower of strength to them all and also went over to see Peter but could get no response. It was he who finally had to break the news "It's over."

"I've always wanted things desperately and then when I've got them I haven't wanted them any more. I feel the same about you." Peter had actually said this to Louise. When Pauline told me, she became agitated, remembering again the acute pain which she suffered when she first heard it; "It's quite horrific to think your daughter has been picked up and then just thrown away."

Divorce was against the family's religious beliefs. They had never imagined it could happen to them. Yet now both of her parents and her sisters were worried that Louise might still try to go back, so they all realised that they wanted her to be divorced. Mike was terribly hurt. He had suffered from depression and Pauline was terrified he might do so again. One of the girls described the family: "We really worked as a team. Dad was so practical, Mum was the comforter. The rest of us were outwardly bright and cheerful, trying to keep Louise's social life going. It brought us very close together." Pauline said it was interesting how they all reacted, from the lively, organising eldest girl to the quietly protective youngest.

They felt wonderfully supported by friends, especially those at church, many of whom had watched Louise grow up. There was a lot of anger, with plenty of advice, usually put quite tactfully. Younger people often said "Give him up, he's not worth it," many more felt great sorrow at the thought of the marriage ending in divorce. Their Christian principles were being tested against their natural impulse to help Louise out of an impossible situation.

All this time their vicar continued to be caring and sensitive. He was never judgemental. He helped them when they were trying to cope with their own feelings of guilt. They often felt they had not done anything really positive and still wondered if they should have insisted on talking to Peter when Louise had said "Please don't." They questioned whether they had taken the easy way out.

The actual divorce settlement brought more unpleasant exchanges, as Peter even objected to the solicitor Louise had chosen, with advice from a friend who was a marriage-guidance counsellor. But he did not want to admit that he had deserted her so in the end they agreed on the grounds of "irretrievable breakdown." Even now he cannot let go. He has moved away but still rings up. He tells her he is unhappy; he talks about his new car, his new job, his ambitions for himself, but shows no sign of understanding or compassion for her. He says now that he regrets leaving her but seems incapable of saying sorry and has never asked her to come back. Pauline still thinks of him with an underlying sadness, fearing that he really has no support at all.

How Louise was helped.

Louise was helped not only by her family but also by the congregation of her church. Pauline said "Everyone was marvellous. She was received as though she had never been away. She came back into the choir and felt that she was part of the wider family once again. People said it was lovely to have her back but they were sensible and didn't gush." This has been a very healing experience for all of them. Yet there are still times when it hurts badly. Louise walked out in tears one day when she heard the Wedding March. Pauline finds weddings difficult to bear.

Mike seems to be able to put his heartbreak on one side and disappears into his own world. He has been incredibly helpful to Louise. They were always good friends. Both parents think that she has done the right thing and admire the way she has behaved and coped with the situation. Louise does not share this view. She has a very low opinion of herself. She still tends to blame herself but cannot work out what she did wrong. She felt for a long time that she was no good at anything, including her work; that she had let her parents down, that everything she touched was affected because she had committed a sin. She also doubts her own judgement of character, asking "Why didn't I see what he was really like?" The family see that their task is to build her up again and give her back her confidence. They have purposely said things like "We did admire you. You never let the side down." They mean it and think that she is slowly beginning to believe in herself again.

Support lines—sharing the pain.

Pauline describes what has happened to their relationships now as "the family coming to the fore." Relatives have been helpful although some of them have been faced with divorce for the first time. Mike's mother, who was brought up as a very strict Methodist, is very sad but has tried to put her own feelings aside because she wants Louise's happiness. She understands that the divorce rescued her from something that might have been horrific, as she sees more into Peter's character. What seems to be a big hurdle for the older generation has not been so difficult for Louise's own friends, who already have a good number of young divorcees among their ranks.

Mike and Pauline have some very good and trusted friends. They are supported by a group who have known each other for a long time. They feel they can talk about anything at all and know it will not be repeated. They think that this is possibly more important than the help they get from their relatives.

Anyone who has gone through the same kind of experience will identify with some of Pauline's emotions and may be helped by her great honesty to understand that they are not the only ones who have such feelings. Many families have problems sharing their thoughts and sadness with each other at such times, but this story shows how parents and children can work through a situation until they are able to do so. Divorce can affect relationships in two dramatically opposite ways. It can result in bringing a family much closer together, with extra sensitivity towards each other, as illustrated here, or it can cause quarrels and unhappiness, which only make the situation worse. How the family copes at the time will almost definitely continue as their pattern for the future.

Not all families will be so involved with quite so many other people; family, clergy, friends and the congregation at their church, but we can see how these contacts can give great support. Pauline and Mike are lucky because they already belong to a close-knit group who understand their problems. Many other parents find similar help, sometimes within their own families.

One mother wrote to me, after her young son's divorce, saying "…I've been really unhappy to find that so many other people have had the same thing happen in their own families. Couples who have been married for four or five years just walk away and say 'I don't want you any more.'" When her sister had the same experience, as her niece left her husband after six years of marriage, she knew what if felt like and understood the great flood of emotion which followed. She writes "It has been both helpful and an added burden to share this situation. I have had to try and listen and support my sister when she has been at her wits' end. We try to understand why both marriages which had so much going for them have now ended in divorce."

Richard and Geoff—father as 'reconciler'

It might seem natural to go to your parents for help if your marriage is in trouble, but couples often prefer to choose somebody who does not know them personally. There are various counselling services and I will refer to some of these in a later chapter. Richard told me in some detail about his family and the support he gave his son during and after the break-up of his marriage. He is an example of how a parent *can* help in difficult times. He summed up the experience with the words "…picking up the bits after my own experience enabled me to help Geoff and understand his problems."

They had enjoyed a good relationship since Geoff's student days, after their family life had already broken down. At that time, four years after he and his wife had been divorced, Richard did not find it easy when Geoff and his girl-friend, Meg, came to tell him they wanted to live together. They both asked "Do you approve? What do you think of it?" Although he did not like the idea he could hardly oppose them. He was still feeling that he had made a relative mess of this own marriage, so he did not want to push them into a similar situation.

He visited them fairly often but was not happy about their relationship. Meg tended to live in a fantasy world, while Geoff had a very quick temper. When Meg announced that she was having a baby they decided to get married straight away. Richard had a long meeting with Geoff, during which he "...gave no encouragement" but he realised they were determined and the wedding went ahead in a registry office, partly because Geoff felt guilty that he had made Meg pregnant when they were not married. The marriage lasted for four years, during which time things went from bad to worse. Meg came from a violent home background and suffered from a series of depressions. There were constant rows as she began to resent Geoff's progress and became more and more angry as she tried to keep up with him mentally.

Richard was desperate, at first, to save the marriage. He felt that if there was anything he could do, he should try. He went to stay with Geoff and Meg for three separate weekends. They talked through their problems very frankly, sometimes to Richard's discomfort, as for instance when Meg told him that she had become pregnant on purpose so that Geoff would feel he had to marry her. She explained her need for security and love.

They tried to see where they had gone wrong. Richard got them to write things down, suggesting that they should concentrate on each other's good points. He felt the very fact that they allowed him into their confidence meant that they did want their life together to continue. He saw himself as a 'reconciler', an enabler, who could help them to see beyond themselves, to stop and think.

This worked for nearly three years. Katie, their little girl, was very important to both of them. As in so many other cases, she kept them together. Richard always felt welcome when he visited them: they trusted him. But eventually things came to a head, through what he described as "...a series of stupid things", which resulted in a tremendous "bust-up", even involving the next door neighbours, who turned against Meg. Geoff finally walked out for the last time.

Man to man support

Richard now put his energies into supporting Geoff, helping

him to find somewhere to live and make some attempt to recover. It was fairly impossible to have any further relationship with Meg at that time, as she saw him as being "...on Geoff's side." Geoff made very generous arrangements for her, giving her the house and a good financial settlement. He wanted to start a completely new life. However, Katie was still his prime concern, so he settled in a new home only three miles away from where she and Meg live. This has worked out well and she has been able to spend plenty of time with both parents.

Geoff's solution to his own unhappiness was to become more and more involved in his work. This situation continued for three years, during which he met up regularly with Richard. They went to rugby matches together and were generally supportive to each other. Richard tried hard during this period to strengthen his relationship with Geoff when he seemed to have no-one, and this has been maintained. He looks back on this period ruefully: the picture of father and son, both divorced, mulling over the past. He found his own failures came up for discussion too. He was told "You still love Mum". He knows that it was all a humbling experience and remembers asking himself again and again "Where have I gone wrong?"

Geoff has now married again. This is a much more mature relationship than his previous one with Meg. Richard is very happy about this marriage. He gets on well with Jean, Geoff's new wife, and so does Katie, who loves going to stay with them. This second wedding took place in church.

Richard was very pleased about this and sees Geoff's gradual coming back to faith as a wonderful thing.

He has never remarried himself. He has always felt sustained by the community spirit of his parish church and the love and care extended to him there. He feels that his own personal and spiritual life has blossomed during the last twenty years and he sees the same happening to Geoff. He understands forgiveness, having both forgiven others and been forgiven himself. This comes, he says, with maturity. He values the help of a spiritual director to guide his personal growth. I asked him how he would describe his life now. He said "I feel I am somehow buying back the past: redeeming the time."

The lessons are very clear. Both father and son emerged from the pain of yet another breakdown of a marriage in their family, stronger and more thoughtful. They built upon their friendship, trusting each other and both learning from the past. The father's own experience of suffering was helpful to his son and his advice was acceptable because it came from genuine understanding of the situation. Both husband and wife had relied on his advice in the past and valued his affection for them and his care for their future well-being.

This might not always be the case, as relationships between the generations are sometimes not so easy. One important factor in this story, which some people might not be able to manage with the same common sense, is the way that they faced reality. When it became clear that there was no possible future together, they got on with the job of organising the best way to live apart, yet still providing opportunities for exchanges when necessary and mutual care for their little girl. Parents should have a good, cool look at themselves if they get embroiled in such a situation. It does not help if they can only think in terms of reconciliation as that may be impossible. In that case they should stay at a distance and help the couple in trouble to find somebody else to help them.

How the wider family can support those who are involved directly.

1. Close relatives of troubled couples, you may need to establish boundaries to protect your own lives and families.
2. Work out how to deal with a situation clearly, or you may get caught up emotionally.
3. Be prepared to realise that sometimes divorce may be the only solution.
4. Don't be afraid to suggest counselling (eg. Relate.)
5. Recognise that newly–divorced people may need help to start again as single persons.
6. Accept that support from friends may be more helpful than from you and the rest of the immediate family.

CHAPTER SEVEN

SECOND MARRIAGES: ACCEPTING AND AFFIRMING

Divorced people often marry again. Men tend to do so more than women. This is not likely to be easy and produces a new set of problems that may take some sorting out, with the result that about four in every ten do not last. Second marriages usually affect many more people than just the couple concerned. I know a number of parents who have found them difficult to accept so I was surprised that nobody wrote to me directly about this aspect and only one person wrote about her experience as a second wife. This led me to seek out people who were prepared to talk to me about how they had managed personally. Once again, I was struck by the open, candid way I was trusted by people who know that some of their friends, especially among church-goers, are embarrassed by their situations. Their stories also show how much they are helped by the love and care of other friends.

I was once reminded that when Abraham set out from Ur on his great journey of faith, he took nothing new with him. He still had all his old pots and pans. I think that simple picture has something to say to those who set out on the journey of marriage, but perhaps especially when it is the second time. Our personal 'old pots and pans' are the past experiences which have made us into the people we now are and they will still be part of us in the new relationship. Both partners have to face the fact that there will be memories, some very painful, which they will not have shared and which must be treated very sensitively. Rachel's story, which now follows, provides us with a rare example.

Rachel and David—marrying a divorced man.

Rachel struck me as a loving, outgoing, capable woman, and as she told me her story, my admiration for her increased. She was a mature student in her early thirties when she first met David. He was ten years older. His wife had left him and taken their two children with her and divorce proceedings were afoot.

There was no doubt in Rachel's mind, almost from the first moment, that she loved him. But they were both practising Christians and his job was very much involved with the church, so they knew that their relationship would be frowned on by some of the people who knew them. She did not know whether they would ever be really free or even, for some time, whether his marriage might not be mended. She believed that he still loved his wife and would have her back if she would come, right up to the final legal case.

Waiting, learning to put up with disappointment and realising that you could not always have what you wanted: these were all familiar experiences to Rachel. It had taken her five years to come to terms with the fact that an accident made it impossible to pursue her chosen career as a gymnastics teacher. But as time passed she came to see it as a strength rather than weakness. In any case, she has a strong, determined character and understands the value of self-discipline. Looking back now, she can say "I knew that being in love might not work out." She sees that period of her life as a growth point.

Once the divorce was over, Rachel and David were legally free and wanted to marry. However, there were many other considerations, not least his children and her parents. His superiors were troubled by the situation and made rules that they should not be seen together in public. They were treated with great affection and very much helped by caring friends but some felt it was the wrong time for David, rather too soon after the breakdown of his first marriage. Rachel felt guilty, in spite of the fact that she had in no way been responsible for the divorce, and had not at that time met Laura, David's first wife, but only wanted to be his wife and care for him. She believed that "…the official line of the church was that divorce was acceptable but that remarriage was the sin." This somehow seemed to place the blame on her. But she was able to feel, both then and now, that she had not sinned in marrying David.

Relationships with David's children.

All the time in the background, there was the question of his two children, both in their early teens, as decisions were being made about their future. Rachel told me that she went through agony at the time, feeling that if they came to him there might not be a place for her in his life after all. David absolutely denied this but she accepted that they had a greater claim and that he loved them very much. She can look back on this period thoughtfully now, able to acknowledge how difficult the situation was. David is a very sensitive man and was very hurt and confused. One of the things which grieved him most was that Laura, with whom they finally stayed, told the children exaggerated stories against him.

They met Rachel before she married their father and got to know her gradually, with other people. At first they saw her as somebody nearer to their own age, who played games with them and was fun to be with. However, once they realised that she would marry their father, their attitude changed. Both, but particularly the girl, wanted their parents to stay together. Once married, Rachel bided her time, having the children to stay for short, regular periods, until eventually they grew to appreciate her for herself. They enjoyed her humour and youthful outlook. All the same she felt that they were sometimes uncomfortable and resented anything they saw as authority in her, acting as their step-parent. This often expressed itself in critical ways: very simple things like comments on cooking or any domestic article that was different from home. The girl seemed to need extra physical affection from David during these visits. He wonders now if this may have been sharpened by seeing his warmth towards Rachel.

Several years on, the eldest is now married himself and the relationships have mellowed. There is a more mature understanding of the crisis which originally plunged the family into turmoil. Rachel has never been disloyal to their mother by discussing her with them but they have come to see for themselves another side to both their father and their mother, rather different from that which had been presented earlier. They treat Rachel as a friend and appreciate her most because they can see that she makes David happy. They have also grown to respect David and Rachel for the standards by which they live. They are both in full-time ministry, giving unstinting time and support to a huge variety of people, in a difficult inner-city area. Their commitment to their work stems very obviously from their living Christian faith. This has actually presented the children with some problems, since their mother's life has been conducted on a very different pattern. They appear to have managed some kind of compromise, taking something from each household.

Rachel feels sympathy for her own parents, whose other daughter has two children, yet they hardly know their two step-children. They are traditional northern folk, who do not express their feelings readily. She remembers the dread with which she approached them when she dropped the "bombshell" that she was going to marry David. There was not only the issue of the divorce but also the age gap. She says that they were "absolutely brilliant" at the time, and did not try to talk her out of it or get angry with her. She had expected an atmosphere of non-communication at best, with her mother going about the house "tight-lipped and buttoned up." She feels now that maybe she did not give them enough credit for their loving acceptance of a situation which they must have found very hard.

Strong marriage.

The marriage, after nine years, has grown ever stronger. Rachel has always been sure about her own feelings but she knows that David had to work his way through hurt, loss and guilt. He saw faults in himself and felt his failure as a father, especially in not being with his children much during their formative years. Rachel also knows that it has been hard for David to let go of his love for Laura after fifteen years of marriage. He feels that the constant difficulty over access to the children was a major factor in the gradual dying of his love for her. Rachel understands that he can never forget the past, nor does she want him to, except for the hurts which have left wounds which she feels have continued to heal gently.

She is afraid that she sometimes rubs salt in those wounds without meaning to do so. She has no respect for his first wife, either for the way she behaved to him in the past or for the way she has lived since then. She tries very hard not to show her feelings but when letters come from Laura, as they do periodically, she sometimes gets indignant and "lets go". This is when the anger which she controlled over her own passive position in the past wells up again. The letters usually suggest the need for financial help, although Laura married again years ago and lives extravagantly, beyond her means. It feels to Rachel almost like blackmail, bringing further anxiety to David and irrational pain to her.

She has no doubts about the rightness of their marriage and does not believe it is against the will of God. It was a sadness to them both that they were legally married in a registry office but they celebrated next day with many of their friends with a wonderful Communion service and renewal of vows.

She has no doubts either about her own work for the church, seeing her original plans and her accident as a gentle path which led her eventually and inexorably to her present ministry. I should add that she asked me to make it very clear that she does not believe in "God-given" suffering or fatalism, since a loving God would hardly bring her to this point by purposely causing suffering.

David has an exuberant faith which communicates to others with real power. His personal experiences have helped him greatly in understanding the problems of other people. Both he and Rachel are much loved by those with whom they work. Their married partnership is recognised and admired, as they are seen to be well matched and supportive to each other. Rachael emphasises that the most important thing is that they are stronger together than apart.

Other Stories

There are some clear lessons to be learned especially with regard to the children. The new 'husband-and-wife team' cannot just set up home and get on with their lives as though the past has never happened. In most cases, the first wife does not simply disappear. Old affections may continue to simmer and have to be dealt with by each of them in different ways.

This will probably be harder if it is the second time round for both husband and wife. Both will have been hurt emotionally and the healing process will be even more complicated. Anne, a divorced woman who has married a widower, says "Nothing really prepared me for this – everything is so different...I miss my friends, my work, my church, my home, but most of all my children. They decided not to come to live with us, but stayed in the north west. They are Christians and are well supported, but it's still not easy."

Her present marriage came after years of unhappiness and insecurity. Her first husband was an alcoholic who was arrested for fraud, broke bail and fled the country. It took many years for her to divorce him, as she believed it was against biblical teaching, so she tried hard to make a one-sided marriage work. Her feelings of responsibility towards her children still torment her. "They begged me not to have him back, but I don't know if they remember that now. I hope not...I don't want them to feel any guilt about the actual divorce, they've got enough to cope with. It was my decision."

Now, she and her new husband are trying to deal with the upheaval and turmoil from her unhappy past and his grief at the memory of his wife's death. She describes him as "a darling man", but says that they are "both rather determined characters, used to acting independently." She knows she is fortunate to have found a loving relationship at this point in her life, but this does not mean the end of problems; they still have plenty to work out, from both past and present. Ann says she would never have survived without a sense of humour and says this, her faith and her friends have kept her going so far. However difficult it may be at times, she is able to say "We do have a great and won-derful God though, and we can really praise him for his love and care of us."

However, it would be a mistake to think that every second marriage has to be terribly complicated. Most of us tend to be amateur psychiatrists at times, so we can easily imagine difficul-ties where they do not actually exist. Some situations are very straight forward and quite friendly. Even when they seem to be fairly complex, this may not be the case, as a great deal depends on the personalities of the people involved.

When I asked a friend of mine, whom I shall call Frances, how she coped with a husband whose first marriage had already broken down after he had left his wife and five children, she seemed to be slightly surprised that I should think she had a problem. She and Lindsey are a couple who "positively enjoy each others' company" and say they "have nothing to moan about". He is a relaxed professional man, now retired, some years older than she is. She is a very practical person with a sense of humour, who does not spend time mulling over emotional issues.

Yet her childhood was very difficult, as her father disappeared to America when she was small, so her mother sent her to a con-vent, with the help of relatives. At school, Frances was a practis-ing Roman Catholic. She remembers her prayer at First Com-munion; "Please God send my Daddy home to me." Sometimes she wanted very much to hurt him because he had hurt them so much. She told me that she always reminded herself "my mother loved him once."

She was happy that her mother liked Lindsey but she knew she was sad because he already had a broken marriage. Most of her Roman Catholic relatives were shocked. I asked her how she feels about the fact that Lindsey still keeps in touch with his first family. She is very generous about this. She knows he loves them. Their mother is a Roman Catholic and has not remarried. Frances says she does not feel responsible for them and describes them as "very loyal children, extremely nice young people" and says she has never tried to be other than a friend to them. They all came to the wedding. They and their little children call her

Frances and exchange cards and flowers and presents. They still come to stay now and then, and are pleased to see that their father is happy. Frances says they enjoy mingling with each other's very different worlds.

It is clear that this is a very firm marriage, with both partners supportive of and dependent on each other. Frances was a very self-sufficient, single woman in the past and now feels "only ambitious in achieving jobs well done." She has made a beautiful, imaginative garden and also enjoys sewing and some cooking. In middle age she is perfectly contented, saying "I don't want only what money can buy." Lindsey goes regularly to his local parish church. Frances is less sure and says that in spite of feeling that her own church has not shown her enough love or care, she "can't leave it for the Church of England because it's somehow still there, underneath the skin."

How parents approach their children's second marriages.

The attitudes that parents adopt when their children marry for a second time are very important right from the start. If they are resentful or very critical, they may live to regret voicing their opinion, as it will probably make it difficult to have a good relationship in the future. People often speak out too soon, before they know all the facts, making it hard to discuss things in a friendly way. Equally, it needs to be said that their feelings are often not understood and they are sometimes labelled 'old-fashioned'.

Younger people have grown up in a climate where frequent divorce and remarriage are common. Sometimes they do not see the pitfalls ahead as clearly as their parents, who will be fearful about the future, especially when an unmarried son or daughter marries a divorced person who may also have children. Remarks made to me include "We were distraught at first...he was our 'baby'...How can she take all that on, three children as well...Will she cope?...It's not what we would have chosen but we told him we'd always love him." I heard of two cases where men went to their brothers to ask for help in facing their parents. Very often, the parents end up devoted to the new family, but it can be hard work.

When the problem is about religious principles it may be even more painful. Basic questions such as whether the wedding can, or should, take place in church are fraught with difficulty. Strict views about the 'indissolubility' of marriage lead to hurt and misunderstanding in the family. I believe that parents have to learn to stand back in these cases, whatever their own feelings. They cannot live their children's lives. I know at least one young person who has never recovered emotionally from giving in to their parents' pleas and did not marry the person they really loved.

It can be quite a shock to parents when they realise that one of their own children has fallen in love with a divorced person and wants to marry them. This is "something that happens to other people...not to us." Often the whole family feels very upset and out of their depth. They may hardly even know whether, or how, to congratulate them. They sometimes get into a terrible state about what to tell the grandparents: should they try to disguise the truth or hide it altogether? Most of all, if they do not already know them, they may dread meeting the new person who is going to be a member of their own family and cannot be ignored. It is very important to establish a good relationship right from the beginning.

I asked one strict Presbyterian father how it had affected him personally. He said "At first I was disappointed. My wife and I knew in our hearts that this was not what we wanted or stood for. But I am what you might call a 'pastoral realist'. I might see the relationship as second best but I can never see people as second best. Our son clearly loved the girl he wanted to marry and we both knew that we had to accept him where he was, while still holding on to the ideal. I felt that he was presenting the cause we stand for in a bad light, as far as our Christian friends were concerned."

When it came to the actual wedding day, he described the ceremony in the registry office as "a form of hell – the absence of all things that mattered about two people coming together." There was a sensitive woman registrar who seemed to understand the situation and conducted the legal proceedings in a pleasant, dignified way. He felt "very devastated inwardly, somehow lost and perplexed, just sad." He said the church blessing which followed "made it better and worse. I was glad it happened but was uncomfortable with it. I went through a whole gamut of emotions: absolute dread and confusion. We somehow smiled through the marriage of 'our baby' while hiding some of our deepest feelings."

He sometimes wonders now whether his 'rigorism' was hurtful to the couple at the time. He and his wife pray for them every day. They have watched them grow into a caring, hard-working pair, committed to their young baby, but without any obvious interest in Christianity, which makes them sad. But they have learned to trust God more as a result, realising that they are no longer responsible for the day-to-day care of their grown-up family.

A mother told me that she looks back on her daughter's wedding day as perhaps the most unhappy experience in her life. She has grateful memories of the kindness of the vicar when they were in the church. He was aware, as perhaps few others were, of the strain she and her husband were under and his sympathetic approach was very helpful to them. The bridegroom's parents appeared to be genuinely enjoying themselves. She did not know them well enough to understand their attitude, since the only time they met there had been no mention of his divorce at all. She did not think (and hopes she was right) that the young couple had any idea how she and her husband felt.

She described how the next day, alone in a quiet church, she was finally overcome by the tide of desolation which she had been trying desperately to keep at bay. She was convulsed by silent, dreadful tears, which coursed down her cheeks. She was mourning for the loss of her daughter, but more than that for the manner of the marriage, which should have been the joyful moment when she moved on from youth to take on the new, real responsibilities of adult life as a married woman. She feared for both of them, having to cope with the problems which they must inevitably face because of his previous marriage. She prayed hard for their future together.

These stories may sound dramatic in some ways but they are fairly typical of what many parents go through. The smiling faces on wedding photographs do not always give a true picture of the feelings behind the 'happy' masks. My own experience at weddings makes me sure that the last thing the new bride and groom need on the day is to feel that their parents are unhappy about their marriage. Sensitive people will go out of their way to make them comfortable and be loving towards them. If they *have* to cry, then they should go somewhere private or store it up for the next day. It also seems wise not to make a fuss afterwards, but to work at building up a relationship without too many emotional undertones. The next couple I want to introduce seem to have managed this particularly well.

Roger and Yvonne—taking on a whole new family.

Roger is the vicar of a large parish in a city in the south of England. He and his wife, Yvonne, talked to me very frankly about how they felt when they realised that their son Michael was in love with Penny. She was not only fourteen years older than he was but was also divorced with two young daughters. Roger said he had found it hard to work out which had made him more upset. He had been brought up from the age of four, after his parents died, by a young aunt "as a duty and without much love," so he could not imagine a married relationship with somebody so much older.

He and Yvonne talked through all the difficulties they could foresee in the future. What would it be like when Penny was forty five and Michael was thirty one…when she was fifty and he would still be well under forty? How would he cope with the two girls? Had he even thought about the problems there would be when they were teenagers? Whatever they said to Michael, leading at one point to a stand-up row between father and son, he refused to see why they were worried and insisted that she was the person he loved and was going to marry.

The divorce issue was a different matter. Roger treats second marriages in church as individual cases which have to be examined carefully. Penny had left her husband and their home on the east coast and came to live with her parents when her second baby was two, but she had never felt able to explain the details of the breakdown of her marriage. By the time she and Michael wanted to get married, the girls were six and eight. Michael had not darkened the church door for some years, so there did not seem to be any grounds for a wedding ceremony there. It finally took place in a registry office, which both parents found very impersonal but Roger conducted a blessing ceremony in the church afterwards, with family and friends and supportive parishioners. Then they all went back to the vicarage for a good party!

In the meantime Roger and Yvonne had gone out of their way to get to know Penny and the little girls, Emma and Jane. They had all spent Christmas together and were relieved to find that they got on very well. Roger decided to be pragmatic. He said, looking back on that time, "There's no point in engaging in self-destruction. We still had our own lives to lead and you can't manage your children's lives for them. I am a priest. I spend my time trying to help people to cope with problems and difficult situations. I find myself very often in the role of peace-maker, so how could I not respond to my own son in his need? I didn't want to put up barriers and neither Yvonne nor I wanted to show resentment or bitterness."

The effect on his work in the parish and the couple's relationship with people in the congregation has been positively good. To begin with, they asked "What will people think?", but they need not have worried. Yvonne was told by a member of the Parochial Church Council "You couldn't wish for a better daughter in law!" She agreed wholeheartedly. Roger felt that their own crisis and the way they dealt with it was helpful, because it made people realise that the clergy are "human" and subject to the same pressures as everyone else. When marriages break up in their family circles they know that he and Yvonne understand because they have had to face it themselves.

It has helped them both in being able to stay alongside other parents in their troubles. Roger speaks of "spending midnight hours with other people in distress. In three out of four cases, children are involved. At least I know what it's like because it happened to us and I know solutions can usually be found, however bleak things often seem to be at the outset."

Six years on, they still have occasional anxieties about the future for Michael and Penny, although they are very happy about the relationship as they have watched it develop. They feel that Michael's comparative youth has made him continue to enjoy his sporting interests more than an older husband might, but he takes Penny and the girls skiing at least twice a year and they have established their own pattern of life. Roger remembers his own childhood "without love" and has gone all out to show affection to the girls. He never thinks of them as "step" grand-children and they respond to his warmth by calling him "Gramps." At one time they all lived together in the vicarage for six months which Yvonne remembers as a very happy experience. They come over as a very integrated family, going on holiday together sometimes, beachcombing, really interested to see where Michael went when he was a little boy. Roger decrees that there shall be "no bickering" (he has seen too much in similar situations) and he seems to be right when he says "in this case there's none of that."

Yvonne says that their relatives vary in their attitudes. Some have been very supportive and accepting, helping Penny and the girls to feel that they really are part of a loving, extended family. But others are less co-operative, slightly scandalised by the age-gap and the open way in which they, as the vicarage family, appear to be condoning divorce and re-marriage. Roger dismisses this as a judging attitude. He is sure that they have acted with compassion in the way Christians should respond to a family in need of sup-port. He said "…we couldn't distance ourselves. We saw the girls as innocent victims of circumstances they couldn't control." He added that in his relationship with Michael the one thing he still stresses constantly is that the girls must not be hurt more than they have been already in the past.

Emma and Jane, like many children in their position, have six grandparents altogether between the two families. They agree that they have got it "all sorted out." They call Michael by his

Christian name, not "Daddy", because they still have a good relationship with their own father and visit him regularly. He has married again and has two small children, a boy and girl. In early days these visits were rather disturbing, as he took them off on fabulous holidays and spent a lot of money on them. Things have settled down since then and the children seem to cope well on the whole.

Yvonne says she has wondered, over the years, what the girls really feel. Her own support for them has been her reliable, unfailing affection. She describes them as loving and very helpful, protective towards their "gran" and their mum. They are learning to stand on their own two feet after the somewhat "over-motherly" care they have received from everybody around them. Penny has found her faith renewed. She teaches in the church school and is an involved and respected member of the congregation. The girls have become teenagers, integrated into the parish, naturally belonging in every way as they have grown up. Their happiness as a family has been a good influence on other people. Roger says it is lovely to see how it has spilled over onto Penny's parents too.

"Very lucky" is how Roger and Yvonne summed up their relationship with Michael and his family. Listening to them, I felt that I had rarely met a less selfish couple. They are a genuine example of people who have applied the Christian faith in a practical way.

How to cope with second marriages.

1. Remember to be sensitive to the feelings of other Christians, who may find your own situation difficult.
2. Be prepared to cope with guilt about the past.
3. Step-parents and step-grandparents need to take time to get to know the children.
4. Parents should not put themselves first when children remarry.
5. It is important for the generations to understand each other's hurts.

CHAPTER EIGHT

THE CHALLENGE TO THE CHRISTIAN COMMUNITY

Christians are criticised for not speaking out about the state of society. We are criticised just as harshly when we do. We are not expected to know about "real" life. The churches are seen by many people as irrelevant, full of holy huddles singing hymns. This is often our own fault. When it comes to the subject of divorce, even though it is so common in our daily lives and fills columns in the newspapers, a lot of church people still treat it as something secret. It is very rare to meet anybody in a church congregation who openly admits to being divorced. The stigma remains, with its suggestion of shame and failure.

Breakdown of family life

Yet when I asked clergy what was the greatest problem they found in parish life today, the majority pointed to the breakdown of family life. They emphasised how much this affected every aspect of their work, especially their pastoral care for individuals. I know churches in city centres where most of the women in the congregation are single mothers, either unmarried or divorced. A vicar's wife on a huge housing estate told me that she often felt she was the only "married" woman in the parish! Not only in cities, but also in country districts, the pattern of marriage which Christians have taken for granted for so long has more or less broken down.

Only twenty years ago, when I was leading a Mothers' Union branch in a Church of England parish, I remember how angry and upset I was when a middle-aged woman was divorced by her husband and "officially" should not have been allowed to continue as a member. I knew that she needed our love and support at that moment in her life more than ever. Thank goodness our organisation saw that need and changed its rules. It was a time when "The Permissive Society", as it came to be called, was at its height. Marriage seemed to have had its day. Living together was beginning to be popular and accepted.

More than just a generation gap.

Young people have grown up in this atmosphere and many of them do not find these views on marriage and divorce strange or wrong. They take their freedom for granted and enjoy it, probably not even aware of how different their lives are from their mothers' experience, since it is mostly due to the contraceptive pill and greater independence for women. Older people have been rather slow to catch up. This is much more than just a "generation gap". Surely no other period has seen quite such a huge change in public attitudes to personal morals during a single lifetime. Some Christians have simply chosen to bury their heads in the sand, comforting themselves that people are still getting married after all.

It is sometimes only when they are faced with reality, because it happens in their own family circle, that they have to accept what is going on all around them. Parents get upset because their sons decide to live with their girl-friends. Then they have to work out how to cope with this new pattern of family life. I have seen an angry father simply disown his son in a fit of rage, with the result that he has never been able to re-establish any kind of relationship with him. Some people apparently do not see it as a problem at all and treat the pair as if they were married. This may cause offence to other Christians. Many parents manage to find a "middle way", keeping in touch with the couple but making their attitude clear when they come to stay by giving them separate rooms.

The people who are least likely to be surprised will probably be the clergy, who have been faced with this problem for years. It is a long time since we saw articles and letters in papers like

The Church Times and the *The Church of England Newspaper* about what to do when a couple give the same address when they come to make arrangements for their wedding.

Nowadays, the clergy know that at least half the people they marry are already living together.

When single daughters become pregnant, parents are involved in dreadful moral decisions, if they are included at all, about the possibility of abortion, which would not have been legally possible in the past. "Illegitimate" babies, as they are still seen, cause endless heart-searching among parents, friends, and especially grandparents. However much love they bring, and they usually do, they also bring guilt to the other members of the family. A friend of mine, taking her baby grand-daughter to the church, in fear and trembling as to how she would be received, could hardly believe it when a woman asked her "Where do you think you went wrong?" That was the very question she kept asking herself.

Today we are having to face problems like that on a huge scale and we cannot turn our backs on them, because they are all about people and relationships. If we really believe we are members of the Body of Christ, then we have to care for the many other members among us who are bruised and try to understand why they are so, without patronising them. It helps to remember "There, but for the grace of God, go I."

Supporting families when marriages break down.

Divorce in church families is now quite common but that does not make it any easier to bear. As I have shown, it is a form of bereavement; it brings deep hurt to each individual who is affected by it personally and it touches everybody around them. Gossip will hurt even more. It is still very difficult for some people to accept divorce at all, if they have been brought up very strictly, so we hear of grandparents who refuse to speak to grandchildren, either because they are divorced themselves or marry a divorced person. I think that families with Christian friends may be helped by sensitive care, but it is important not to swamp them with too much obvious sympathy. A letter or card, gently letting them know that you are remembering them in your prayers, may be enough. Friends who know the family well should be ready to listen. They may have no answers but that will not really matter. Some people will find it easy to share their feelings openly with other members of their church, while others will be more private people who find this difficult.

Clergy are often drawn into these situations, as we saw with Louise in chapter six, where the vicar was a great support to the whole family and even acted as the "go-between". In this case he already knew them well. It can never be easy, but sometimes it is not so obvious how best to help. Some families will find it very embarrassing, particularly if they are on the fringe of church life. However, it often happens that people get to know each other and build up trust through these experiences, which can lead to a closer friendship and eventually to them becoming committed members of the church community. The most important thing to remember, when dealing with a family's shock and grief over divorce, is not to be judgemental.

It is also important for church members to realise that the clergy are not trained social workers, in most cases, so they will sometimes be affected personally by the traumas of people they know well. So will their families. Sue is a young clergy wife with a small baby. She told me how upset she was when her husband had a phone call to say that their youth leader had left his wife. "I was in the bath. I just couldn't believe it. I jumped out and rushed straight round to them. The boys were crying and their mum looked terrible. I put my arms round them all and found I was crying too. Then Sam, who's only ten, stood up and said 'I've done my crying…now we have to face the future and decide what to do.' They had just collected the photos of their summer holiday. They all looked so happy on them! When I left, Sam said 'Well, I suppose I'll be like most of my friends at school now, without a dad.' It broke my heart to hear him." Sue and her husband had been planning to include that whole family in a special preparation weekend away for their confirmation candidates. They have gone on caring for the wife and children, having them round at the vicarage, helping them to face life on their own. They have also been in touch with the husband and tried to "repair the damage" but to no avail. Sue said "You can't just shut off your feelings. We love this family. We worked with them. It hurts us too."

These kind of problems happen in clergy families as well. In the last chapter we saw how Roger and Yvonne coped with their step-grandchildren. I was told about a vicar and his wife whose daughter's marriage came to grief. The congregation at their church, who had known her as a girl, were very loving and supportive to her parents. One of the family described them as "superb". But the church where she worshipped herself "viewed her as a 'leper', not young enough to be in the youth group, but a danger to married bliss in the Bible Study!" She felt totally rejected and her parents were very upset on her behalf. They eventually helped her to find a church where people were more understanding and she was able to set up an informal group of friends with similar problems. Yet even there, she did not feel that her difficulties were really understood by most of the congregation until one day when her ex-husband rushed in and behaved appallingly, trying to abduct their baby from the church creche. Then they had their eyes opened.

When a vicarage marriage fails.

Christians often put their clergy on a pedestal and want them to be perfect, so if a vicarage marriage falls apart, it is usually seen as more serious than any other. Certainly, the effects will probably be very far-reaching and can be extremely damaging to the community. Not long ago I had the sad experience of visiting two parishes where this had happened. In the first, the affair which the vicar had with a parishioner had hit the national press a few weeks earlier, so there was no secrecy. It was a Confirmation and the vicar's eldest son was a candidate. Members of the congregation were wonderfully sympathetic and understanding. They rallied round the deserted wife and children with genuine affection. It seemed to bring out the best in many ways, although there was great sadness too.

The second occasion was actually more difficult and fraught with intense emotion. A young, much-loved couple simply left their parish without any explanation, without saying goodbye. The bishop, affected personally by the tragedy, had to tell the congregation that the vicar had resigned. I shall always remember that service; the shell-shocked young families, the sad-eyed older women, the numbed, lost faces of the men, the feeling of shared pain and guilt. Somehow, we all took on the responsibility. We acknowledged our own failings. The lesson was from Job 38:1–21 and 42:1–6, a marvellous passage which reminds us how small, how unimportant we are. We pleaded with God, singing:

> Bend us, O Lord, where we are hard and cold,
> In your refiner's fire, come purify the gold.
> Though suffering comes and evil crouches near,
> Still our Living God is reigning, He is reigning here.

So we could at least end on a note of triumph! My husband and I say the *Savator Mundi* (Saviour of the World) in our chapel almost every morning. Since that day, remembering the fervour with which we said it then, I have offered it for the people of that parish.

> 'Jesus Saviour of the world, come to us in Your mercy:
> We look to You to save and help us…
> Come now and dwell with us Lord Christ Jesus:
> Hear our prayer and be with us always.
> And when You come in Your glory:
> Make us to be one with You in Your kingdom.'

After the service people told me how they had been helped with their own marriage problems by the vicar and his wife. Some of them still found it impossible to believe that they had gone from their lives for good. The elderly felt it was like a bad dream, but when they woke up in the night it was still there. The young desperately wanted the couple back. But I felt they understood better than most congregations would have done twenty years ago.

I have had several letters during the last few years from clergy who have been divorced, and in some cases have remarried or have married a divorced person. They realise that, compared with conditions in the past, they are fortunate to be able to continue with their ministry. However most of them have found that it is difficult to move to a new post, often because the people do not approve of their married status. They find this very hard, especially as in some cases the people who interview them have been divorced themselves. It does seem to be unfair but no doubt it reflects our need to feel respect for them. I could not find an easy answer to the question put to me by one parishioner. "How can a man who has not kept his own marriage vows explain them to a couple when he is preparing them for their wedding?"

Marriage preparation

"Couples coming to marriage preparation groups seem to think that marriage is made in heaven! They simply don't seem to realise that anything could go wrong for them." That was the verdict of a minister who still goes on trying to get couples to understand what they are taking on. Some clergy have given up or have never started. A few years ago I was a member of a working party on marriage preparation. We sent out questionnaires to over 300 clergy. Only about a third bothered to reply. There were all kinds of schemes, plans and ideas. Some were very ambitious and well organised, with different speakers over several weeks, including such people as a doctor and a marriage-guidance counsellor (now Relate). Others consisted of one talk with the vicar. The fact which depressed a number of clergy was that so many people move away from the area after they are married and the contact is lost. Maybe it might be worthwhile to work out a system to let clergy know about them beforehand, in the place where they will be going to live.

A vicar pointed out to me that a lot of couples who turn up at his vicarage have never darkened the church doors in their lives, so it is easy to get cynical about marrying people who are not regular parishioners. The importance of what are known as the 'Occasional Offices', baptisms, weddings and funerals, sometimes jokingly called 'Hatching, Matching and Dispatching' is often debated in church circles. I think they should be seen as a marvellous opportunity. Weddings in particular, which are such a mixture of solemnity and joy, should be very special occasions. They are very special for the families concerned, so it really matters how the minister conducts them. They are probably the time when the ministry is most "on show" to those outside the church. If this is a good experience, it may help people to dare to try coming back. It also gives an opportunity to make contacts with the couple's families, which can be followed up in the future. Some clergy say they suffer from "wedding fatigue" when they have to conduct too many, but it is just as well not to show it!

If the minister does not want to be involved in preparing couples for their marriage, apart from the essentials of the actual service, there is no reason why members of the congregation should not take on the task themselves. There will be plenty of people with experience, some of broken marriages, who will be able to introduce some realistic discussion about the pitfalls and snags which may lie ahead.

A friend who works for FLAME (Family Life And Marriage Education) suggested that although marriage breakdown is not usually mentioned directly in preparation groups, perhaps more attention should be given to it. In any case, now that a number of weddings take place where one partner has already been married before, it is not really possible to ignore their previous experience. Even the practical details make this necessary, such as what to do about the other half of the family who will be coming. This can be an embarrassing problem. Quite a few of the people who wrote to me mentioned having children from their first marriage as bridesmaids. But perhaps I should add that several others, mainly children, said they had not been able to bear the idea of being present at their parent's second marriage at all.

What is a family?

In 1988 the bishops of the Anglican Communion from all over the world gathered in Canterbury, England, for the Lambeth Conference. I was privileged to be there too, taking part in the wives' conference. One of the issues which dominated the discussions during those three weeks was the subject of the family. We in the West were very aware that family life in our part of the world was generally becoming very unstable. We knew that the American scene, from which many of our own country's values seem to have percolated slowly, was even more shaky. However, we got plenty of surprises. We heard delegates from Australia in despair about the state of marriage there. The Africans were even more upsetting, when they described how their extended family system, which we thought was still secure, was breaking down all over that continent. Among the statements which were made as a result of the conference, the one which many of us regarded as vitally important read:

"We believe that the family, whether a unit of one parent and children, an adult and an elderly parent, adult relatives, a husband, wife and children, or whatever other shape, is the fundamental institution of human community."

FLAME has taken this seriously. It is a voluntary charity working through the dioceses of the Church of England. It's aim is "to support and sustain education in family life, marriage, and the whole range of human relationships." The very fact that such an organisation exists, and that its workers' conferences and workshops are used more and more, shows how much Christians are having to face the real truth about family life today. It is very down-to-earth in its approach. An example of its message to a generation brought up on explicit sex in the tabloid newspapers and on TV, is that physical love is not usually what messes up a marriage. It is more likely to be a problem of communication. In other words, couples need to keep on talking to each other...and to their kids. Perhaps all some families actually need to learn is to turn off the TV a bit more often!

Divorced women in middle age are one group which FLAME

tries to help particularly. They are often cut off and lonely, staying at home and avoiding other people. It is hard to go out socially on your own when you have been used to being one of a pair. It is often hard just to go to church, even if you have plenty of friends there. The feeling of rejection can be so great that confidence simply oozes away. I was helped to understand, at least a little, how this can feel, at a conference on marriage and family life led by Dr. Jack Dominian. I was in a group where everybody except me was single, and half were divorced. They all said they found the emphasis on "the family" in their churches made them feel left out, because they came to the church alone. They wished there could be a more positive effort to stress the value of the church community as a family.

This is where the rest of us come in. Members of organisations like the Methodist Women's Network and the Union of Catholic Mothers have a great role to play in giving each other mutual support. So do those of The Mothers' Union to which I have belonged all my married life. It was started in Victorian days with the aim of strengthening marriage and family life. That has not changed but we have had to adapt to the present climate and now the last of our five objects is the one most quoted: "To help those whose family life has met with adversity." It was interesting to see an article with the title "What is a Family?" in the MU national magazine Home and Family, by Christine McMullen, (Sept 1993) which to some extent echoed the Lambeth Conference statement. It caused a huge outcry from people who felt it was an attack on traditional marriage, which shows how far we still have to go to understand what has been happening to our society.

There are plenty of other caring organisations, among them the "Acorn Healing Trust", which trains Christian Listeners, and "Care for the Family". Others are listed in the back of this book. A project which originated in America is making headway in the Roman Catholic church. It involves "Rainbow" groups, which are set up to support divorced and separated Christians. They have a very positive emphasis and each group has a chaplain. The work has developed with "Rainbows for all God's Children", which is an attempt to help children who have been bereaved through death or divorce.

Traditional church groups may not appeal to parents who are bringing up children on their own. It may be easier to join one like CLASP, which was founded in 1982, "in response to the need for Christian single parents to share together their difficulties and blessings." CLASP stands for "The Christian Link Association of Single Parents." Members believe that the healing power of Christ is the lasting answer for those who feel isolated and damaged by broken relationships or bereavement. As this association has grown, it has been able to help people to establish some local groups, which meet for prayer and discussion and may organise some social activities. There is also a penpal scheme. I was interested that this was mentioned more than once in letters I received. In one case, membership of a group ended in a new marriage!

The International Year of the Family

Each year some cause is adopted by the international community and given a high profile. 1994 – The Year of the Family – got tremendous publicity. It started with a great hullabaloo in the newspapers, the TV and the radio. Perhaps this was the result of panic and hopes that at last something might just possibly be done to stem the tide. The Christian community seems to have taken it very seriously, if the numerous conferences and piles of literature are anything to go by. But the real work must be done by each one of us as individuals, in our own family circles and local churches and groups. To quote from the Archbishop of Canterbury's address to the Mothers' Union (3rd Nov, 1993) we must help "not in a judgemental spirit but in a spirit of deep compassion."

The churches were the centre of community life in the past, when most people lived in villages. In the broken world of our day, we can still offer a sense of "belonging", by caring for the lost and the least and the lonely, those who desperately need to be included, accepted and affirmed.

How the Christian community can help those suffering because of divorce

1. Consider the attitude in your own church towards people who have been divorced.
2. Re-assess whether your church concentrates too hard on the family, without emphasising the family of the church.
3. Use members of Christian organisations like The Mothers' Union, The Union of Catholic Mothers and The Methodist Women's Network. They can be effective carers in cases of marriage breakdown.
4. Work out how to educate church groups with help from organisations like FLAME or CLASP.
5. A congregation would benefit greatly by group study of the report "Children Living in Re-ordered Families." (Social findings Policy 45; Joseph Rowntree Foundation, The Homestead, 40 Water End, York YO3 6LP).
6. Collect the ideas circulated during the International Year of the Family and use them to set up local support groups in your own community.

ORGANISATIONS AND GROUPS WHICH MAY BE OF ASSISTANCE.

CLASP – Christian Link Association of Single Parents.
FLAME – Family Life and Marriage Education.
Care for the Family.
The National Step Families Association.
Relate (Marriage Guidance).
The National Council for One Parent Families.
Gingerbread (and organisation for single parents).
CAB – Citizens Advice Bureau.
Families Need Fathers.
Rainbow Groups.
Centre for Family Research, Cambridge.
The Mothers' Union.
The Union of Catholic Mothers.
The Methodist Women's Network.